Hope, Certainty, and Faith

Cycle C Sermons for Lent and Easter
Based on the Second Lessons

David Plant

CSS Publishing Company, Inc.
Lima, Ohio

I0142797

HOPE, CERTAINTY, AND FAITH

FIRST EDITION
Copyright © 2024
by CSS Publishing Co., Inc.

Library of Congress Cataloging-in-Publication Data (Pending)

Names: Plant, David (Pastor), author.
Title: Hope, certainty and faith : cycle C sermons based on the second
    lessons for Lent and Easter / David Plant.
Description: First edition. | Lima, Ohio : CSS Publishing Company, Inc.,
    [2024]
Identifiers: LCCN 2024031538 | ISBN 9780788031199 (paperback)
Subjects: LCSH: Bible. Gospels--Sermons. | Lent. | Easter--Sermons. |
    Common lectionary (1992). Year C.
Classification: LCC BS2555.54 .P497 2024 | DDC 252--dc23/eng/20240802
LC record available at https://lccn.loc.gov/2024031538

For more information about CSS Publishing Company resources, visit our website at www.csspub.com, email us at csr@csspub.com, or call (800) 241-4056.

e-book:
ISBN-13: 978-0-7880-3120-5
ISBN-10: 0-7880-3120-1

ISBN-13: 978-0-7880-3119-9
ISBN-10: 0-7880-3119-8   PRINTED IN USA

To Grandma Plant

She would sit beside each of my siblings on her piano. For each of us, it was a time of joy as we shared in the secular religious music, played with gusto, as her bright red fingernails clacked across the keyboard.

My other siblings reported a similar but different encounter with her sharing questions and ruminations of all kinds. For myself, in one of her 'thinking aloud' moments was the following. "I wonder if there will ever be a preacher in the family who might go to the church in Katy Lick (WV) and share the good news in front of the stained glass window with the Plant name on it?"

It was a memory long forgotten until one day, at a clergy retreat, the presenter shared that he felt all of us in the room had been named to being a pastor. That memory from my earliest of years came flooding back. Perhaps it is so.

Now as a grandparent I am forever mindful of what I say, how I wonder in front of my grandchildren and I can't help but think of those bright red fingernails that played in the saloon on Saturday night and the church organ on Sunday morning. O what joy they wrought. May it always be so.

Contents

Introduction

There are several things that can be helpful to you as you read this small book. First, my personal style of preaching is relational in nature. By that, I mean I preach without a manuscript and in most of the churches I have served, I do so from the center of the chancel area or even down below the chancel area. I will often change or modify my message based on the reaction or interaction I have with the worshiping community. This means that even as developed, in manuscript form, these messages have a more informal tone to them; they require your imagination to fill in the gaps, especially if you are more of a manuscript preacher and wish to add more of your exegetical background research. With every church having a unique character and sensitivity to worship, I encourage you to think creatively, for examples that might reinforce the overall concept you wish to achieve. I used the New Revised Standard Version, 1990, published by Cokesbury, text by Graded Press as my primary text unless otherwise noted.

Second, my own preaching is always contemporary in example. What that means is that I would always be using timely examples from what is happening in the week I am preaching. That is a challenge for a project like this when today's news: war in Ukraine, Israel/Hamas, immigration border issues, and the beginning of a presidential election cycle would normal fill some of the "application" pieces that I would add. I did not include a lot of those simply because they may not even be close to what is happening a year from now. But by not using them my sermons are likely a little shorter than I would ordinarily preach and leave you lots of room to expand.

Third, I never look at the message as being independent from the whole of worship. In some cases, the 'other' parts of worship are critical to informing the message. For instance, I like singing so I am keyed into the value of hymnody as both a reference point as well as effective lead-ins to preaching. And for those more able than I, use of contemporary music via video or drama via video is critical. I might make a shout out to the Bible Project for excellent telling of scripture in a contemporary way. It lets me say less while folks remember more. So too, I am also fond of the congregation reading the scripture responsively with me in its entirety or using a key word responsively that reiterates an important point that will be made throughout the message. Do use a variety of resources to make sure that the complete worship encounter has value to all who experience it.

Fourth, my introductory message for the Revelation readings says a lot about where I come from in interpretation of scripture. To be clear, I don't ever remember Revelation being in the cycle before and even if it was, I would have stayed away from it just on the grounds that it's difficult to help folks work through the complex imagery and possible meanings of it. I find it challenging enough to just help them understand what Jesus was talking about sometimes, let alone a prophetic book like Revelation and its other worldly imagery. Yet, I did take the challenge willingly and hope you too might take an opportunity to dig into it in ways that can enrich your congregation's life. I did find that as I worshiped in Advent, many of those hymns would make good hymns for the congregation during a series on Revelation. You might look for links between your Advent messaging/services in 2023 and worship with your efforts on Revelation.

Fifth, I did look at the 2025 Lent and Easter season Epistle selections as ripe for preaching in a series format. As always, each church's traditions vary regarding the use of the lectionary readings on a Sunday. I do tend to be a single scripture preacher on a Sunday as a habit, so series preaching is easily doable. My testimony is that two to three times a year, sermon series are great opportunities to drive home important points. I am not afraid to send home homework as part of the preaching. Educators understand the basics: repetition is critical to learning. The average person takes about fourteen repetitions (think back to how you learned 1+1=2) before a concept is learned deeply. That means sometimes a person gets the idea in one hearing, others 28. With fourteen being the average, a sermon series that has unified preaching themes, unified musical themes, and both physical manifestations of the concept needing to be taught from body movement to choric speech or responsive readings, and more, you just might get to the necessary repetitions for whatever it is you are trying to impart. Much depends on your space, how creative you might be, the support structure of your staff, either paid or volunteer, to bring the kernels of the text to life in multiple ways. Yet since this is not a worship development book, I leave a lot of these 'other' pieces to the worship puzzle to your imagination, but my own style never leaves the messages' words to themselves. They are always surrounded by other sensory engagements as part of the whole worship experience to drive home the point.

Finally, if I truly believe that all preaching is highly personal, then I expect you to read what I have (I suggest you always read it aloud regardless) since that is how I dictated it and then do with it what you will. May God receive the glory and may the words of my mouth and the meditations of all our hearts be acceptable in God's sight.

Ash Wednesday
Second Corinthians 5:20b--6:10

Being An Ambassador

This evening we are celebrating Ash Wednesday. You may or may not know that Ash Wednesday is not practiced by all Protestant congregations. Many people know it from our friendships with people from the Catholic church or some of what we often call "high churches". As we begin our Lenten journey this Ash Wednesday, we find that the Epistle readings throughout Lent will be the focus of all our services. The readings contain a call to evaluate our relationship with Christ and how that relationship lives its way out through our witness. A common theme in our Epistle readings is that they help us to navigate the waters of self-reflection and service to Christ.

You will find that sometimes the Epistle readings will start with a call to action, or a description of who we are to be and what we are meant to be, how we might behave. Sometimes they begin with the affirmation that Christ is Lord and that we must focus our energies on understanding what that means in its fullness and its complexity while at the same time finding ways to make it real and practical in our everyday life. And what we find in these readings for the next weeks is the proverbial preacher's advice of: tell them what you're going to tell them, tell it to them, and then tell them what you've told them. Throughout these weeks the themes will be robust, regular and deep. They will test us, and they will push us in areas that might make us uncomfortable. They will remind us about the heart of faith: What is it you believe about Jesus the Christ, and how is it that you live that out in your daily life?

Today's reading is a reminder that the end result of faith is not accomplishing a journey to heaven but about being a living, tangible ambassador for Christ. It is a call first and foremost to remember that being an ambassador requires that we are to work on ourselves and who we are in light of Christ. We can't be an ambassador without engaging the important understanding of what following Christ means and having a clear understanding of how we articulate that in our daily moments from minutes to years.

To be an ambassador starts with asking a question "what am I supposed to be / do as an ambassador?" You and I know the word ambassador mostly in relationship to those people who represent our country in various places around the world. We call them ambassadors and we are hoping that they represent us well. We don't know much about how ambassadors are chosen or what their criteria is, we just know they exist. Ambassadors play a critical role in promoting their country and serving as a country's exemplar of its ideals.

They help to promote values, to interpret the public conversations in the media, to navigate the sometimes-challenging waters that citizens face when visiting foreign lands, and oftentimes they help those who would wish to come to our land, to obtain the necessary paperwork whether just visiting or hoping for a more permanent status. Sometimes we hear about ambassadors when war breaks out, or the worries of war, and then they become a means of helping us to understand what is happening in a foreign land. There is much more to this basic understanding but if we think about it as a means of representing the interest of a country in all its complexities it can give us a good understanding of what is ahead for us, and what should be our role as ambassadors for Christ. Note that this scripture does not put this out there as an optional request. Unlike ambassador postings on behalf of a country, Paul said we, all of us, are called to be ambassadors and it is to be our life's work.

If we look at the passage from Second Corinthians, it lays before us the depth of obligation and responsibility that we carry. Tonight, we are not going to go into detail about all those things we must be about doing but we must understand that Ash Wednesday reminds us of the importance of commitment. It reminds us of the depth of commitment required and reminds us that *that* willingness extends to following Christ even into enduring and difficult situations.

Second Corinthians words lay out the challenges that are ahead. Being an ambassador means that we understand the centrality of our importance to sharing God's word in the world. It says in verse 20 we are ambassadors for Christ. (read verse 20) Did you get that? Since God is making an appeal through us, we become an important part of letting people know of God's presence. Just as an ambassador represents a country's interests abroad, we represent God's interests to everyone that we meet. It is reminding us that people are watching how we behave, how we talk, how we act towards one another as a sign of the appeal of or the lack of appeal of God's interests.

Further, this passage talks about endurance, afflictions, hardships, calamities, beatings, imprisonments, riots, laborers, sleepless nights, hunger, the practice of purity, knowledge, patience, kindness, holiness of spirit, genuine love, truthful speech, and the power of God as things we must practice and things we must engage in if we are to fully live in harmony with God. I have no doubt that some of these give you pause, and you might decide you want to reconsider being an ambassador for Christ. But the final verse reminds us of the worthy end of all…the chance to possess everything.

Each one of these foci are going to be reflected in the variety of readings the epistles offer throughout Lent, so this evening we are not going to spend more time on the particulars of each or how we achieve them. This evening we are reminded of what we are signing up for. Frankly, just as the training was long to help the early followers of the Christ appreciate what they were being called to do, we too know it is not something that is going to be done in a moment or in only a few worship services. It is not something that is going to be completed once and for all. But we are reminded that we are a people called to be ambassadors. Just like in the real world of being an ambassador for a country, it requires skills, understandings, and depth of exploration that only come through dedication and perseverance.

One of the key components of this Corinthian reading is to remember that the greatest caution is to remove from us those things that put obstacles in other persons' ability to seek God. Lent is about that. A self-examination of what is causing us to be an obstacle that keeps people from seeing God and renew our lives in such a way that people see in us the very thing they are searching for and want to be part of. Therefore, we are called this evening to begin the challenging work of defining what our ambassadorship looks like and to make our commitment to being the best representative for Christ that we can possibly achieve as a human being, as a participant in this world's ways, as an ambassador for Christ. We make the commitment tonight not only to say yes to our weeks of reflections, but to also pledge our commitment to follow Christ, wherever that may lead.

Amen.

First Sunday in Lent
Romans 10:8b-13

Saved For What?

I am always amazed by scripture and how just a few verses can contain so much. The scripture before us has some beautiful images in it. For instance, from the start of verse 8, the second part, represented by the b in our scripture reading, it talks about how God's love language is so close as if our lips and heart are involved. It is a sentiment that is full of richness, full of assurance that in our believing, in the living of our days and the proclamation of life we are surrounded by a word that is near us and rests in the very being of our body. As we go into the next couple of verses, we are reminded that what we believe and live out, is that God took death and changed it into resurrection and that because of that action we are renewed, saved. Similarly, as we head into verse 10, it reminds us that our confessions and the proclamations of our mouth, are so critical to the living of our days. There is no distinction the scripture says between peoples, that God is generous to all.

Verse 13 brings with it, besides the affirmation of being saved, questions: saved from what? saved for what? That phrase just rolls off our lips and it is one that is critical to our understanding of the faith. I think it is to help us understand that I, you, each of us, is in a state of salvation, both done and not yet done. It is a call for us to honestly reflect on whether we have fully embraced the gift of love and sacrifice which Christ brings to us and in like manner calls us to live out. It is much like the decision to have children and say I am going to accept the completeness of what it means to be a parent. It is like the commitment we make as a grandparent, aunt, uncle, or a godparent during a time of baptism, we are called to say God here I stand, I pledge myself to you, I wish to accept your challenges as my challenges, I wish to accept your way as my way, I wish to let my heart be moved in such a fashion that it will turn from those things that are creating brokenness and hopelessness and instead find in it a robust love that passes all understanding. We are saved from a sense of inwardness around only ourselves to a sense of outwardness toward God and all within God's creation.

I once served a church that had a husband/wife couple that, if there was any family that we would ever point to that would have every possible reason to hate God, to think of God is cruel, to think of God as unreasonable, to think of God as not answering prayer, they surely would have had reason to reject God. One was always sick or in the hospital. We would joke about the reality and when I would visit, particularly the husband as he was the one most frequent in the hospital, so much so that he was almost always in the same room, even the nurses joked that the room should be named after him. The few times his condition was in a state of balance sufficient that he could go home, his wife would then fall ill. I'm confident that the reason she would fall ill is she would spend so much time taking care of him that it would exhaust her body and exhaust her own sense of ability to be of support, the helpmate that she wished to be. Because of the constant turmoil in their lives, they lived in a small broken down mobile home that needed many repairs. They lived on the edge financially. They were constantly struggling with piles and piles of doctor's bills. Yet in it all they maintained a sense of holiness, a sense that they were under the care of God. They felt saved, even if they did not know what for other than their firm belief that they could give their testimony that God was seeing them through these difficult times.

That kept them earnest and their striving to be close to God through their readings of scripture, their prayers, their continuing love for one another and for God through all things. Their lives never changed. God did not suddenly give them a bounty of healing or a bounty of riches or a bounty of great friendships that would go out and raise funds for them. But they had a bounty of faith; they had a bounty of understanding that salvation is about the ordering of one's heart to be in harmony with God. Interestingly, even as they thought what faith they had was not sufficient, for myself, I thought their faith was a great testimony, perhaps even more so than most of the other thousands of members I have ever served, they gave a life of pure devotion to praising and loving God.

We are saved by the fact that we can find ourselves in the midst of the greatest trauma and yet find ourselves in a place of peace, a place of hope, a place of certainty because God is with us. And as scripture gives its own testimony, that nothing can separate us from God's love, you note it is always freely offered, merely waiting to be embraced. Every faith tradition teaches a different way to understanding the business of being saved. Some Christian traditions say you must fall on your knees confess your sins that you're unworthy and like the song "Amazing Grace" we need to confess that we are wretches before God. Then request, 'God save me'. For others it is about understanding that we are powerless without God. Like the Alcoholic Anonymous testimony that says we are unable to do anything without the strength of God behind us, freeing us from the bonds of alcohol, reordering our lives, perhaps not in the radical way of the monks in the monastery who order every second and every minute in the hopes of fully proclaiming themselves one of God's followers but rather in the sense that when we arise in the morning we are able to say this is your day God so that at the end of the day, what we have done may be to God's glory and honor.

Each tradition offers different ways to gather close to the understanding and practice of being saved and to what we are being saved. But the point of them all is to enable us to sit is a place of 'saved-ness', a place where we are close to the heart of God in all things. Part of our Lenten journey is to challenge ourselves, to examine ourselves, and dig deep, asking a bold question about our own reordering of our lives. Are we fully committed to God's wonderful grace and are we letting it in to every corner of our lives. What are you saved from? What are you saved for?

These questions that I raised, saved from what and saved for what, have been implied in my comments up to this point through some of the examples I have shared. Let me again go back to Ash Wednesday's message that our first and foremost task is about us being an ambassador for Christ. If people don't see God in you, then you are not, in my thinking, representing God's saving actions fairly. Simply feeling one is saved is not sufficient, however comforting it might be. It might be in our hearts, but what about on our lips. This suggests that we must become better at our public affirmation of faith, not so much having to stand on a public square like the Apostle Paul did proclaiming Christ but, sufficiently enough in our lives that people will say thank you, I know God better through you. Perhaps this is why I have always been close to the AA work.

What starts the journey in AA is the recognition that one needs to be saved from the addiction to alcohol. For those who proceed deeper into the program, they realize that what they are saved from is far more complex than just giving up alcohol. It is about recognizing the intrinsic tumult of their lives that began before their drinking and was exasperated by their drinking. That they need God to help them understand that the condition they seek to change was part of the choices made and that now, with God's help, they can seek different choices that involve healing, mentoring, confession, making amends, and constant diligence in searching their lives for the things that draw them away from health. But even in this model, the affirmation is still within the confines of a trusted system of confidence. Is that our only option?

I had gone up to the zoo with my family and because my knee is bone-on-bone, all the walking meant at the end of the day I needed to sit down on a bench. I found a place off to the side. I sat there rubbing my knee and a gentleman noticed and he came by and asked if I was okay. I shared my knee was just bothering me; that it was an old injury and that day it was just swollen and feeling aggravated. He asked if I was able to get up and get around and I said, 'Oh yes thank you, I just needed to have a moment of sitting instead of being on my feet, until my wife comes back from shopping in the museum store.' He asked if he could pray for my knee. I told him that he most certainly could pray for my knee and that I appreciated his thoughtfulness.

Perhaps, if I had been thinking about this message at that time, I might have said to him that I appreciated him being an ambassador for Christ. It was a simple action on his part, not unlike the action that when you maybe stop and you see a person off the side of the road or in a place and they are thirsty. You offer them a bottle of water; you don't just hand them the water, which is what good people do but you hand them the water and say 'here take this bottle of water and know that I give it to you in the name of the Christ the one who gives living water.'

You see, God saves us not just for ourselves. Even the couple I was talking about earlier who just had lives that were so full of distraught and challenging things found great comfort in the faith but even more importantly when they would be at church they also gave testimony and sometimes that testimony was about what was happening in those hospital rooms and the kindness of the nurses who they would converse with and then they would ask if they could pray for that family. Or the joy that they would celebrate when it came time to give a small gift to the church out of the meagerness that they had, and they could proclaim how much they appreciated all the love and support they received.

Sometimes in Lent we try to think about the big things. Arrogance, greed, sloth, and all sorts of words that connotate major issues (and certainly some of us need to address those), but most importantly I think it is about us getting our heart right with God and being able to share that news with each and every one through the everyday encounters we have. For most of our encounters with the world are small and tiny, like that little bit of mustard seed that is talked about in scripture. It is about that small act of love, of a gentle hand upon the shoulder (or a knee) that brings comfort. It is a word reminding others that God loves them too, and has saved them. Perhaps those are the greatest works of all for we who are saved, we become a people of generosity, a people of humility, a people of gratitude, a people of praise, a people of loving our neighbor as we ourselves would wish to be loved. That is what I think it means to be saved and for what we are being saved for. Remember, you are an ambassador for what you believe. Be it for Christ in every way that you can.

Amen.

Second Sunday in Lent
Philippians 3:17--4:1

Words Matter

One of the key things we learn in the movement from reading a passage to applying it, is the tendency we have to think that the author is speaking about someone else, not us. What I am suggesting, whether we like it or not, our first, and perhaps best landing place in a scripture is to start with the presumption that the one being picked out as the worst example, is, indeed, an image of us.

This may be harsh, but it guards against us thinking that surely, we can't be the ones who are falling short. After all, we are here, in church, faithful members, giving our tithes, our time and talent. We carve out our time for Bible study, prayer, Sunday school, worship, and fellowship activities. Surely not us? Yet…really? Can we honestly say that our minds aren't set on earthly things like our bellies mentioned in verse 19? In our case, as Christians, the message of the good news is a reminder that we succumb to the tendencies that the things of this world are our focus way too much, and that our lives are, too often, and with blunt assessment, a humiliation, before God.

For example, when I examine the cars in the parking lots of churches, are some of them not a real tell-tale sign that our minds are set on earthly things? I know that as I get older there is always a tendency to try and compare one generations' cost to another's. But I do wonder why there is a need for a vehicle that costs $88,000 versus one that can transport just as adequately for $28,000. The other vehicle may be nice, lots of room and versatility, but isn't it exactly the indication that, in this case, an earthly thing, has caught us? Same with our houses? There was a time when we shared rooms with our siblings, and the single bathroom was the norm. But things transitioned. Everyone thinks they have to have their own room and no less than 2 1/2 bathrooms are the requirement, a great room, huge kitchen, and more, even if most of the space was never used during a 24-hour period. Of course, as churches we have little to be proud about. Most of our buildings are used a couple hours a week at best. The $1,000,000 investment used by a couple dozen people, and even more disgusting is that the justification is that the space is "sacred" or "holy", as if God really prefers his rooms to be empty six days out of seven.

Am I being too harsh here? I don't think so. When Paul tells us that our humiliation is upon us, it was a pointed and judging statement to cause us to come up short in our exhortations of our innocence. He reminds us to make all things subject to Christ. All things, all things.

Let's get more pointed. When we devote weeks, months, to our "house" projects are they really being done in the spirit of subjugation to Christ? When we want that 55-inch screen tv are we really doing so in the spirit of subjugation to Christ? For instance, when a church I once belonged to decided that it was better to spend $100,000 for a new church organ rather than addressing the issue of race relations because, well, 'we can't get involved', are we really doing so in the spirit of subjugation to Christ? Or when another church really hated the fact that a preschool was using all the rooms of the building, providing the church with $40,000 a year in rent, but, gosh darn it, it's terrible that their materials take up so much space in the classrooms that the church kids use on Sunday mornings for an hour. Is that really the spirit of subjugation to Christ? What about the church who lovingly offered their building for a week, once a month to serve as a sleeping shelter to the homeless but of course, just had to install locks on the sanctuary so 'they' couldn't use it because its sacred space.

My wonderment is where is the real holy space in that building? The rooms housing the beds, the bathrooms providing a place to wipe down, go to the bathroom, or the room separated off by locks? I know that the church people would think the sanctuary was, indeed, the holy space, when I think we all know Jesus would think the rooms with mattresses on the floor were really the holy spaces. Perhaps the pews would be better served if they were converted to beds.

Folks, do I need to get more pointed? Any advertisement you see is trying to tell you, put the world ahead of Jesus. Most everything you have, you had the option of buying, or adding to, is an encouragement to put the world ahead of Jesus. Much like we try to help our children understand the difference between want and need, the reality is Jesus, through Paul's admonition, is asking us the same. And frankly, as adults, we generally don't do any better answering the difference between want and need than a first grader.

The playpen we live in is big and full of distractions. Paul is asking us to keep an eye on the ball. What are we really called to do, to be? Paul was clear, subject yourself to the Lord. Subject all your life to God. Like all Lenten messages, this requires serious self-examination. It requires a discipline to conform ourselves, for example, to change our lives so that they are ruled by different priorities than what the world teaches us should be priorities. I think it is time to ask ourselves to do some serious soul searching both individually as well as corporately.

First, what do you have that reflects glory to God versus glory to yourself? What kind of time do you invest in those self-interest glory things versus doing the things that give God the glory? How might you transition the things of your life, even your own life values/habits so that they align more closely with Christ's principles?

Second, assuming that as a regular church goer you know the values that Christ shows us, things like personal disciplines of prayer, scripture reading, worship, presence with strangers, feeding/clothing the naked, doing the prisoner visiting thing, doing the healing thing. How might your personal life reflect/live more of those things?

Third, let's think about our church. This wonderful space we worship in. How is it sacred when it is only used an hour or two a week? How might we turn it on its head so that it is used every day, every hour? How might our building, the work of our church, more effectively use all this property for God's glory? Even now, with so many churches trying to reinvent their building for a more entrepreneurial use, is it still done too often in a self-serving way, to gain money so we can keep going rather than being done in a way that is responsive to the values that Jesus exposes as our primary reason for existence. It is not the idea that our space should be used that is the problem, it is how our space is being used and for what.

And finally, what of our vision and mission of our church? Does it really conform to what Jesus asks of us? Too much of what we consider vision and mission is another way of asking how we might get more people to help pay the bills so that we can continue existing, rather than understanding that when we do as Jesus asks, it will all take care of itself, maybe here, maybe not. If our building, our congregation can no longer serve Jesus' purpose, and it folds, so be it. If it thrives here or somewhere else, so be it. But at least we will be doing as Christ asked.

And when Paul makes the pointed statement about our humiliation we can, hopefully, truly answer that it isn't us. Because we will have owned it and decided we needed to change so that we can give God the glory.

Amen.

Third Sunday in Lent
1 Corinthians 10:1-13

What's In A Habit?

Here we are on our third Sunday in Lent. The stage has been set with the last few Sunday's messages that we are being called to look closely at our lives; for the places where we are falling short of the intended life Christ wishes for us. Most of the scripture sampling around this theme so far has been focused on generalities, even as those generalities can be pointed in their accusation that we are falling short. You are still here, so now we start to drive the point home with specifics.

First, let's acknowledge the reminder in verse 13, that nothing we are talking about is not also common to all. While it may not lack irony that we are all in the same boat in a land that glorifies individuality, we should take comfort in the assurance of scripture that we can find the way out if we are so willing.

The first complaint that Paul leveled was that we spend too much time at the dinner table and at play. Given the fact that we have, post Covid, returned to the many pleasures of eating out for instance, or going to the movies, shopping, vacationing in droves, we tend to view too many of these things as just the normalcy of a regular life. What the implication of this, is a self-centered form of indulgence. Because it's there, because our culture is wrapped around things, we want them. We don't really need them, we want them. One of the financial gurus complained that one of the reason middle class folks are stuck in a financial rut is that they spend five dollars for a cup of coffee at a drive through. He suggests that is pure indulgence, not valuable if you are looking for security. And note, he was not even challenging the many and varied ways we expend resources on any number of choices of beverages when water flows unabated from most of our taps. Indulgences are real.

They become commonplace when, in fact, they are illusory of a bankrupt system that convinces us we must have something when little of it serves any useful purpose other than distraction or dependency, entering the dump after our deaths. Not only can we not take it with us, but no one else wants it, either.

The second complaint that Paul leveled was sexual immorality. Well, this was, and is indeed, a great problem. From human trafficking in the sex trade, to the vast amount of porn that is viewed everyday by "good" adults and unwitting adolescents, we are replacing natural desires for companionship and closeness with momentary pleasures that isolate us from one another. We succumb to it in ways both graphic and subtle from clothing to misplaced emphasis on what a sexual relationship should reflect, to relationships based on gratifications rather than responsibilities.

The third complaint that Paul lifted up was that we whine insistently about the supposed restrictions the faith places upon us. I have often thought that an excellent Bible study should be called, "Wine and Whining", a look at the extravagance that runs afoul of God and then the incessant complaining when it goes wrong, whether the complaining is to blame another, or it is somehow unfair to be punished for it. I must admit, I always winced when church members would come back from an extravagant vacation and talk in detail about its pluses and complain about its minuses while I had just spent a week trying to keep a single mom from being evicted from her apartment. Or even worse, whine when it came time for the annual stewardship drive that they can't possibly give any more all the while planning their annual cross-country trip or inviting me over to see their new 55-inch tv. Are you a whiner? Do you have much but whine about its toll on you? Perhaps we need to rethink what we are doing.

Paul, as always, didn't leave us with only a chastisement, he said Christ "provides us with the way out". While he didn't list the how, we know that the way out is often the reverse of the condemned behavior. Overly stuffed tables and lavish dinners are to be replaced with not just humble tables, but tables filled with strangers needing their first meal of their day or perhaps the last taste before death. In other words, tables that involve others, not in a night out for those who can afford, but in service to those who cannot.

Immorality comes in many forms. While I don't think we have to move toward a puritan or conservative notion that sex is only for procreation and without meaning other than for the purpose of procreation, it does mean that looking at the other must include something other than our sense of using them for pleasure. Immorality is blunted by a deep relational concern for the other in our lives and is to be seen as an extension of the caring, loving gesture of putting the other first, desiring an intimacy that comes from knowing one another (in the sense of fullness of personhood) before the knowing of the other (in the sense of sexual gratification). It becomes too easy to use Paul's caution as a means of denying our sexual yearnings. But its caution is that it is far too easy for us to let those yearnings rule us in a way that diminishes the other.

The extravagance of whining comes from having so much that we somehow feel inconvenienced when it doesn't go as planned. Since some of you know of my enjoyment of golf, I often remind myself when a round that goes bad that it is not an excuse for whining. After all, I often quip to myself, 'remember, you could be having to travel ten miles with a bucket on your head to fetch water or wood'. And it is humbling, to say the least, to put this activity that gives me exercise, fellowship, and dare I say pleasure, a deeper look, becoming aware that it might have a longer term impact on environmental issues than I would care to really consider. While I am still not sure if my point of self-reflection about it is adequate when I justify the activity as a means of engaging a lot of other people I would otherwise not know and use, those engagements provide a chance to give my testimony of faith and pastoral encouragement in the conversations that often occur. But, is it enough? Paul challenges me too.

The bottom line is that Paul wants us to take a hard look at what we invest our time in. Specially noteworthy are the issues of outsized abundance at the table, our sexual morals, and our complaining when we have it not so bad. Paul would never say that life is perfect in any fashion and since he was often bereft of specific details on how to behave in certain situation, he simply, but deeply, reminded us that our lives must be understood as reflecting God, and that others are watching (even if we think they aren't). All failure on our part becomes a shortcoming to all. All applications of Godly principles therefore become a success of all. We shouldn't shrug off the significance of that.

Therefore, your homework this week is to look closely at how well you are confronting the issues identified in this passage and begin the journey toward healthier ways of living. Let's start with taking an inventory. Pray: walk into each room of the house or your apartment and ask a question. How much of what I have do I need versus what I want? What does all this space, all these things say about myself and what I am devoted to? Where does Christ fit into this? Where should Christ fit into this? Similarly, take an inventory of how you spend your time. What are you doing with your minutes and your hours and your days?

When Paul spent so much of his letter writing time to chastise is it not his hope that we might take seriously a realistic examination of our lives? Not just for the purpose of rooting out that which holds us back, but rooting it out so we might make room for that which can be better, enriching not only our lives but enrich the lives of others through the saving grace, peace, and love of Christ Jesus our Lord.

Amen.

Fourth Sunday in Lent
2 Corinthians 5:16-21

Labels Everywhere

It is hard for us to function without labels. When Paul began this section with the summative "therefore," he asked us to regard no one from a human point of view. It seems to me that what he was trying to put forward was a concept of not using our regular categorizations of persons, think descriptive, or political, or titles, or definitions of occupation, and the like. What he did do was go on to talk about that those who were in Christ as new creations. He returned to the image of ambassadors for Christ as he had brought forth in the readings from Ash Wednesday. Today, more than ever, I appreciate the hardy affirmation that he wished to make on our behalf: that we need to move to a point of delabeling ourselves from all those things connected to worldly points of view and instead connect ourselves to the one who we call Savior. That is good news for all.

This is a hard thing to do even in those situations where the emphasis is on the new. I return to thinking of my friends in AA and my family members who have been in Alcoholics Anonymous as they attempt to reconcile themselves and their past behavior with their new sense of personhood. Their group gathering conversations include a common refrain. It goes something like this at AA meetings: "Hi, I'm Dave and I'm an alcoholic. But thanks to God (or higher power), I have been sober x number of days." Then the person will often talk of their story filled with language of their fall into alcohol, their shortcomings, and the pain their lives caused others. Then they turn to the sense of new life that they have but that seems forever colored by their label, 'Hi, I'm Dave, and I'm an alcoholic.' The label, even if no longer shared as a negative, still lingers over every aspect of their lives. It is not unsimilar to the faith traditions that always start the revival with, "Hi, I'm Dave and I am a sinner before God."

One of the central parts of the AA meetings is that they always work very hard to talk about the means by which they continually address the shortcomings of their lives and the pitfalls that remain because of their disease. They are always supportive of one another and the ways by which they might continue to live sober. I won't go into greater detail but one of the principles of AA contains an accounting for what one has done and ways by which one might address that with integrity, honesty and an understanding that new life is a choice. This is a choice that comes from purposeful decision, from commitment, and that comes from deep abiding honesty about who one is to be. A good part of the understanding is that one's life is not defined by the bottle but defined by one's life being linked to God and claiming that that link is the path to staying sober. Yet the confession, the label lingers…I am an alcoholic. For an outsider of AA, it might be difficult to understand that that 'label' is both a word of confession and a word of victory.

Similarly, Paul was trying to help us see the end game, if you will, of the Lenten journey. Yes, we have been called to rigorous examination of our lives this Lenten season. Yes, we must like alcoholics, account for our addiction to worldly things however they manifest themselves in our lives. Yes, our accounting must be thorough, and must take into account all that our lives have impacted. It must include all the things that come from seeking our own pleasures and how they have displaced us from a living of our days that God intends for us. But that is never the end of the story in either an AA meeting or in the epistle's hope for us. Did you do your homework from last week? For Christians in discernment regarding their lives, regarding their sins, to use the classic word, regarding those things which have kept God distant the epistle is saying to us that the end game is to rise beyond the 'sin' label and put on new behavior remade in the image of an ambassador for Christ.

As we explored earlier on Ash Wednesday, being an ambassador is a call to a complete devotion to the ways of God. It is as if we have signed up to enter a monastery with full attention paid to every detail of every moment but rather than doing it only within the four walls of a building or a set aside community, we are called to be an ambassador in the world. That world is our neighborhood, that world is our nation, that world is all those ways we interact within God's created venue. Therefore, again in the spirit of a Lenten theme we are encouraged to see ourselves, in every moment, engaging in Christlike activity. There is no formula for how to do that other than the complete and full focus of our lives on the intentions we bring to each moment.

A new phrase that is in our lexicon of contemporary culture is mindful living. Seeing each moment as an opportunity to be aware, and in soul language of the church, faithful. Similarly, like the AA participant we cannot help but recount the past because it is a harbinger for similar situations we are likely to face today. But part of that recounting of the past is also the recounting of the day we decide to go a different way, and the steps already taken toward a new way of living.

That was what Paul was similarly indicating to us when he talked about becoming an ambassador; when he talked about overcoming that which has been to become something new, something different. It is not that everything that has been is completely, forever gone, but rather that it takes its rightful place in our story telling. I was lost but now am found. I am a sinner but now I am an ambassador.

Even as I began this message with my head nodding to the desire to put away labels, at the least, we can recognize that the journey that leads us to those one-word descriptors, can never be fully contained by them, even as we might try. Yet perhaps it is worthwhile to attempt to do so. Hi, I'm, well…a human trying to put on heavenly things. Forgive me when I fail…encourage me when I succeed. Let us walk together in this journey of being more holy for God's sake as well as our own.

Your homework this week is to now move away from making the list of things done poorly, that get in the way of godliness and begin to think about how they might be transformed or replaced by things that lead to a life worthy of an ambassador. Begin to list out the things you intend to put your time into that aren't of the world, but of God. Like AA, put them into a list of steps that you can rehearse every day. Further, find someone who might hold you honest to your intentions, someone to partner with in your attempt to be more holy. "Hi, I'm Dave. I'm a sinner but now I am an ambassador for Christ, seven days into faithfulness."

Amen.

Tell It Like It Is

Friends, part of a critical understanding of the faith is that we must be willing to give our testimony. Testimony is an old word that we don't use much except in the court of law. Paul's injunction to us was that, rather than being about a specific "testimony" on a particular action, he wanted to help us understand that our lives are living testimonies. He wanted us to practice that living testimony both in word and deed.

One of the things I always liked about the scriptural witness around the letters attributed to Paul is that he was always quite up front about his own shortcomings, his own struggles, his own sense that he has or had special privilege. He also was forthright about his continuing struggles to remain faithful to Christ even as he admonished and gave instruction to others, attempting to mentor them through the hardships and joys of being a faithful follower of Christ.

The scripture today starts out with his own sense that if anyone had a right to brag about where they came from and who they were, he certainly would have had a right to brag. Yet, as we know from his story, he quickly became a person who understood that the world that he once affirmed and believed in so strongly, that he felt confident he could go out and be judge, jury, and executioner to those who had fallen by the ways of the faith he so adhered to was a mistaken application of the faith. He realized that none of that had any value for him in the way it once did. Whatever he had he viewed it as gone, no longer relevant, and no longer being of value to the way he wished to live.

I think it is important for us to understand that Paul had a certain amount of hubris in believing that what had been did not affect his current way of thinking. But that didn't mean that the goal he was ascribing to here was not worth our consideration. For example, as much as I wish to and desire to be fully open to other persons, other ethnicities, and other countries, I still am bound by certain parameters of place and people: realities that I know can box me in. That they hold me back from being as full a representative of Christ as I would wish to be. Over the years, as I have opened myself to other points of view, I have been convinced of the reality that my past does continue to enter in as I work to process the information of life that is always coming at me. And while I would like to assume I am free of all those past thinking and living errors, I can't really claim with certainty that I am. Like Paul, I know that not only did I fall short but will continue to fall short unless I stay alert to those things that weigh me down as well as replace them with the things that will buoy me up to be ever more faithful, in a healthy way, for the sake of our Lord.

One of the current themes in our culture is the way we look at gender and our bodily identity. Today I might use language that I didn't know existed even fifty years ago. I will be, and am forever bound by being an American, white cisgender male. I lead a middle-class life fairly free from the torments of the vicissitudes of life that many have, at least to the degree of impact others might have who are extremely poor, or medically broken by illness, or psychologically broken by our system that fails to aid people in finding a path to wholeness. While I have great empathy for others and have listened to many stories and absorbed them, taking them to heart in the hopes that I can be more fully sensitive and embracing in ways that are helpful to those that I meet, I know that my experience is bound by the place and time of the living of my days. Even as I might understand with some slight measure what it means to be food insecure, or homeless, I certainly have no real way to comprehend devastation of the kind that refugees face or those in the war zone experience. My own experience may have led me to parts of a city where gunshots are heard during an overnight retreat, but I doubt it really compares to a situation of continuous bombing, moving around, trying to find any small morsel to eat, or fresh water to drink. I find it so easy to get lost in the jungle of emotions and intellect where we are unable to break free from the sinking feeling that it is all too overwhelming. Yet, Paul encouraged us to keep our eye on the prize, being faithful to Christ, so that in the end we are joined fully with him, in both this world and the next.

This Lent we have been encouraged to examine ourselves. How well do we represent Christ's values and dreams for us, a hope that we can be ambassadors for a faith that is demonstrative, in every moment and every action, a reflection of Christ's life? I have shared with you ways you might think about your life and yourself through several 'homework' exercises or lifted up stories about people who have overcome any number of things and yet continue to give God the glory.

Now it is your time to give your testimony. How would you write the opening paragraph of your life in the same spirit as this short passage from Philippians, which, as well as any, might describe Paul's life? I remember from a spiritual retreat, years ago, to contemplate what I might have on my tombstone. To write down what I would hope that others gathered at my funeral might say. Of course, this wasn't an exercise to try and proclaim with certainty what life would bring or even if someone else might actually be able to encapsulate, even me, what my life meant. But it was an exercise that was designed to help me and the others at the retreat to try and capture our story of faith. And in capturing the story, be more comfortable with sharing it with others.

In my career as a pastor, if I find one thing above all others, lacking in the people I serve, is that they can't articulate their faith story sufficiently enough to share it. Early in my career I thought it was about people just being humble, but I came to realize that they just didn't ever really go through the examinations, the crisis of conscience, the active reflection on the meaning of all they did and are doing as someone like Paul had done. Not for the purpose of either feeling disappointment or gratitude, but for the purpose of realizing that their life has meaning for those that they touched, and that their life has had a fulness of experience with God that others need to hear so they might also believe.

Giving testimony is something that requires some form of preparation and practice. Paul wasn't born a writer/orator. Paul wasn't born an evangelist, first for the law, then for the good news. He practiced, shared, and honed his experience, putting it into words, after countless interactions with others who asked questions, or challenged the meaning of his words. And if I believe in the importance of testimony then I believe it valuable for you to invest time in the telling of your story of life and faith with intentionality so that you too might give your words and wisdom to one another.

We don't learn to pray, to read scripture with depth, to share sage advice without doing it. We do it first in the simplest forms and then layering more and more upon it. Why is it that if I ask for someone to pray over the meal, most reject the offer? Why is it that if I ask someone to stand to talk about their reasons for giving, they say no? Why is it that when I ask someone to visit in the hospital with me, most say they would feel uncomfortable? Is it not just because they just haven't practiced it enough to become confident that their own story of struggles and faith affirmation is worth sharing?

As we are coming to this last Lenten Sunday, I ask you to think about this. What if every one of you was confident enough to lead prayer, or make a testimony about your faith journey, or find comfortability by offering a helping hand to others? Do you think a bunch of church folk like us, everyone being able to do it, might find a means to reaching out to others and encouraging them in the journey of getting closer and closer to God? We have had a lot of 'homework' to do this Lent. I did think about giving you some more for this week. But perhaps the ultimate nod to Paul this final Sunday is that you note these few verses in Philippians are all about him, his struggle, his goal, his testimony. Perhaps that is sufficient for us to leave today with its application to you. What is your testimony? How would you sum up your life of faith? Can you put it in eleven sentences? Perhaps that is enough of a task for now. I won't ask for anything else. But I do guarantee that if you work at it, you will find a new way to be an ambassador for Christ that brings a joyful glee of closeness to God that is not otherwise achieved in any other way, whether in this life or the next.

Amen.

Palm Sunday / Passion Sunday
Philippians 2:5-11

The Burden And Joy

I must admit that Palm Sunday is one of the "special days" of the year that tends to make me feel ambivalent. The way we celebrate it tends to get ahead of the story when a scripture is chosen that makes the good news of Christ a done deal. It is the classic dilemma of a 2,000+ year old church that has retold the story of Christ over and over. But Palm Sunday, by its very nature is not a good news story. Especially the way that our reenactments go with celebrative music, palms waving, children processing. Lots of joy, little introspection. We want to *feel good*.

However, this is the problem when we try to incorporate reenactments of scripture into services without benefit of the actual context in the hearts of people. To be most valuable, our enactments need to find ways to incorporate the insults, the false praise, the hope for a rebellion, freedom from tyranny, fanciful expectations that God is miraculously overthrowing despots. We, as a church, give little time to the betrayal and death that will take place in short order; the original story of a shallow crowd, praising one minute, abandoning the next is left unaddressed. Even the liturgy of the past that calls this Sunday, Passion Sunday or Palm Sunday, is mixed in its intentions.

When we march down the aisles with waving palms, are we prepared to examine our own shallowness and betrayal of Jesus that shortly follows? Will it be enough to simply mention that Jesus coming in on the donkey was a clear snickering at the pomp and circumstance that the earthly "kings" thought they had, and that earthly people tend to mistakenly take to mean that their way of solving the problem of an overlord is really just doing the same, but only with one of their own? When we celebrate by singing great hymns of how children sang, or how hosannas rang out, or that Christ has come and read a scripture like this, that assumes a complete understanding of who Jesus was, are we not skipping the turmoil of his passion week filled with betrayal and death? The words of verse 8 are almost a yawner of affirmation.

Bravo Jesus…you humbled yourself. Can we get on with it now, we know the story, let's get to Easter now. Especially since we might not be in church next Sunday as its Easter break in the schools.

I don't mean to be harsh here, but if we let Lent go, and we let Passion Week fly by, we are like the proverbial "preaching to the choir'. Bottom line is, if the church weren't already filled with those who have a churchly habit, even if only on special holy days, would these words mean anything to anyone else? Paul, after all, was "preaching to the choir". He was talking to people who had already rehearsed the story over and over, and Paul's writings sound like a well-edited doctrinal or dogmatic position already made certain. Now don't get me wrong. I think a lot of the church year in Protestantism is a yawner without much joy. I really don't want to contribute to the problem of today's church which is perceived as being drab, boring, and without joy. But why choose a day for a reenactment that isn't fully honest in its depth, and the hypocrisy of which, in the next few days, will become etched in the deep memory of the church and its practices? Perhaps we need to spend the vast majority of other Sundays having a parade, joyfully celebrating, but perhaps not Palm Sunday. Yet here we are…and frankly, I doubt the 23 churches I have served did significantly better under my leadership in changing the culture of our shortsightedness. They liked it the way it was, and I didn't stay long enough in most of them to change that dynamic which reached even beyond Palm Sunday. But that doesn't mean we shouldn't try. Let's take a look at the epistle today, perhaps with a little more demanding eye.

Philippians starts with Paul praising them for all that they have done for him, for others, and that is their virtue. They were living witnesses. How do we lay something alongside our "Music Man"-style parade to better engage the fulness of the story without throwing it fully under the bus as my opening remarks might seem to indicate?

I think we need to start with verse 5. It becomes too easy to just rush by these few opening words. It seems to me, that this is the very point Paul was most eager for us to hear: for us to have the same mind that was in Christ Jesus. Let me say that again. We are to have the same mind that was in Jesus.

First, Paul was worried that our minds weren't synced up with Christ's. It puts a spin on the fact that we likely haven't taken the form of a slave, verse 7, that we haven't humbled ourselves, verse 8, that we haven't been willing to both figuratively and literally die for Jesus, verse 8b.

Second, Paul wanted us to get our act together. When he asked us to spread the word about Christ so that every knee bends, guess what, he meant it. Not figuratively, like leading a good life. But literally, getting our butts, our hands, or feet, and our mouths in gear to actually talk to others about the faith. To actually act in manners that are suitable for those who wear the name, Christian, Christlike, inviting others to do the same.

Folks, the pageantry of Palm Sunday is for show only if we aren't willing to lean into the life that Paul, an ambassador for Christ, is insisting we adopt. The journey we have been on this Lenten season has kept after us regarding our lagging and tardiness in giving ourselves over to Christ. As much as we might want to have a triumphal parade announcing our arrival, Paul just won't let us go. Paul won't give up on reminding us of what following entails: complete abandonment of all the worldly things we have come to know and love, perhaps even the cute kids parading or the halfhearted or even maybe enthusiastic waving of palms as if that really shows our character.

Our character will be shown in the meals we serve this week to the hungry. Our character will be shown in those we visit who have been imprisoned or our willingness to stand on the picket line protesting the next capital punishment victim. Our character will be shown when we provide a home for, dare I say it, an 'illegal immigrant'. Our character will be shown by who we are willing to abandon after all the pomp and circumstance is done and we choose to abide by 'don't say gay' or 'don't make me uncomfortable'. Yeah, I'm sure Paul didn't mean any of these things. After all, probably as a 'slave' to Christ, we can, in the words of a presidential candidate last year, learn some useful skills to provide for ourselves. But I seriously doubt that that is the fullness of spirit Paul had in mind for us. Maybe for a politician, but not for a faithful follower of the Christ.

Have I driven home the point yet? Palm Sunday should make us nervous, very nervous. I am one preacher not willing to let the Lenten part of the last weeks let us off the hook so soon. Since I know most of you won't come to the other services where we talk about abandonment, betrayal, and brutal death of Christ's story, and our continuing part in it, Paul reminded those he was writing to and now us, that we just better not let it slide by. Even on a day like today with all its pomp and circumstance.

Friends, Easter comes soon enough, can I implore you to linger awhile longer over the tough hard truth of following Christ and the demands it puts on our character? We can still celebrate, can't we? We can celebrate that Christ has reached us in time. Soon enough to be a living witness to that which brings real meaning to life and those we touch? When we do the hard work of self-examination, like Paul's words from last Sunday when he judged everything he had done before as worthless, it is a reminder that something else has replaced what was worthless. What replaced it was what is good and right. If anything, that is why we should parade and celebrate, acknowledging that Christ's ways of humility, slavery, abandonment of sin, complete devotion even unto death, yield life changing, community changing, world changing results. In that sense, we do become ambassadors for Christ, a title I wish for you as you adopt it for yourself having done all the hard work of Lent. Perhaps that is worth a little palm waving, if only for the Christ who implores us to follow? Perhaps it is worth a little palm waving for the effort given so far but never with the notion that it is enough?

Fellow sojourners in faith, it is not for me to judge your heart, but it is my responsibility to ask how your heart has entered into this season of Lent and how it is being moved to be yet closer to God. Our Lenten introspection has come to an end, now the practice of following Christ begins, as we enter the fullness of passion week, and exit on the other side as those who would call ourselves, Christ's followers.

Amen.

Maundy Thursday
1 Corinthians 11:23-26

A Time To Remember

You and I have shared these words or words like them for all the time we have ever been a part of church. Even when I was doing jail ministry, I found that most of those incarcerated knew some form of these words. Is it merely enough for us to share them once again?

It would be a legitimate action to take. There is an assumption that the words bring comfort to us because they are familiar in our liturgies of the table, whether we practice them occasionally or weekly. They are a retelling in Corinthians, of a central tenet of the faith. Jesus came, Jesus taught, Jesus died, that we might know a new way of living, and that remembering proclaims this very gracious act of God on our behalf.

For those who have had me as their pastor, I always include in my Maundy Thursday remembrance a nod to Jesus' foot washing act for his disciples (usually with hand washing), as well as an expanded confession experience as a sign that we acknowledge the betrayal of Jesus by humans represented by Judas at the table and then the denials that come in the garden during the later evening, early morning hours. Often, my liturgy for Maundy Thursday suggests a story being told, unfolded, with provocative scene explorations, moving from the typical painting like masterpieces that show a rather stilted form of eating that distances the original participants in a linear fashion, to considering a more family table style meal. And finally, if the sanctuary allows, I always serve the communion, using intinction style, where everyone either comes up to the table to receive the gifts of the table individually or they are taken to individuals not able to come forward, unless I have been able to convince the church to hold the meal around tables in a family style setting. I do so because I think it drives home the point that Jesus' meal was very much, eyeball to eyeball, whisper to whisper, human voice to human voice.

I mention this because for me, the simple words of this setting remind us of the intimacy Jesus had with his disciples and by inference, we are to have with one another. Paul, in the few verses preceding our passage was pleading for the church in Corinth to rise above their divisions that have led them to not engage in a meal of family but in a sort of picnic that has everyone eating in their own time and place when gathered, unresponsive to others gathered.

Paul wanted the Corinthians to rise above divisions and reminds them of the place of the gathered meal as central, a place of communal oneness that overcomes divisions. Sadly, I must admit that Christendom has largely fallen short in this regard with our divisions over this 'sacrament' in that its interpretation, frequency, style of remembrance is at the very heart of the reason why some don't gather together for worship in a spirit of oneness. Instead, we gather in our own church's suggesting that the way *we* do communion is the right way. Paul's calling on us to remember is a plea, not just for our church members but the church universal to remember. Christ wants us together, at the table.

Even as we serve the sacrament today, do the hand washing, or have confession I know that there are some who aren't here because of 'division'. Whether because of culture or simply liking things the way they have always done them. They don't like change or any of the reasons why change might be helpful. It is too personal. It isn't what they are used to. They don't want to hear about betrayal or death. They would rather have warm, fuzzy recollections rather than the clearly unsettling full story of that night with personal bickering, chiding by the teacher, angry leaving, depressing intimations of the finality of the days ahead despite desperate pleas to say it ain't so. But the lectionary reading does not go into the belly of these few verses with all that proceeds and follows this passage. We who preach know the Corinth story. You who have long been in the church know the fuller version of the story. But here, Paul simply reminded us that this table, its remembering, its proclamation is that Jesus died at human hands but still, Jesus claims us as *his* children. The choice is ours to accept it or reject it.

Paul's urgency in these eleven chapters into Corinthians, should be a sufficient warning to remind us of the centrality of Christ to the life of the church. It suggests that too many people don't fully remember anymore. The breath of the Holy Spirit that once settled upon all those left behind on that fateful day we call Pentecost, seems already to have slipped into near oblivion in his timeline much like it has in our timeline. But the remembrance, Paul said, just won't let us go. Paul reminded us that he won't let us go either because Christ won't let us go. Could we also be in danger of falling away? Could we, too, be accomplices in betraying Jesus by deserting him in front of others, not living up to his practice and life of servitude?

I will end with a nudge to suggest you look up a song by Bryan Sirchio. He was a very popular musician back with in my youth ministry days. Bryan has a song, "The Table of Friendship and Love". In that song he talked about a youth not fitting in anywhere, who went on a church retreat. He was tired of the divisions in his local school, the nerds, the jocks, the in folks, the out folks, and the like. The youth decided to go to lunch one day, sat at a table, and put out a sign: 'A table of friendship and love'. They all came, one by one and found common community in a simple witness about a table open to all. You can find the music on YouTube if you wish.

Paul, like Bryan's song, and like Jesus, asks us… to remember. Remember the table as being that which reminds us of whose we are, and who we are to follow, and for what we are created.

Amen.

Good Friday
Hebrews 10:16-25

Confronted By The Cross

A dear friend of mine, a scholar, will soon receive his Ph.D. in his studies of the early church. Far be it for me to compete with his being able to learn most of the ancient languages so he could read the earliest texts and make clear distinctions between authentic and that which is not. Being young in years, he is unafraid to just say it like it is. He often was clear that Hebrews is a book of the Bible that most all scholars concur contains little of value for us if we are looking at good, exegetical preparation to inform our preaching. It contains little that can be tied historically or theologically to the actual thinking of the early church.

I don't want to go into detail about why that is so or how it likely made its way into our Bibles, or even now, why newer translations don't simply remove it or rather, make it clear if this view of my friend is truly a consensus. The fact is, it continues to be before us and as preachers before me note, our task is to take what we are given. If you apply modern day sayings like, "make lemonade when handed lemons," or any other type of saying indicating a seemingly implausible situation then here I am, suggesting a way to deal with this passage assigned by the lectionary.

I have already stated as the first responsibility…pointing out the likely fictitious nature of this scripture so that we understand, that at its best, we can say that our interpretation must be cautious. Being mindful of its unknown origin, it can only lead us so far in trying to uncover its usefulness to us in the living of our days. It is sort of like turning on a news show, and they show a clip of something that happened, and then spend multiple hours trying to tell us everything behind the scenes that they think something means, when in reality, they are guesses or possibilities to what is behind the words or scene we just saw.

Let's be clear here. It's Friday of Passion Week. We have gathered to remember the brutal death of Jesus. The foundation of a concept of servanthood and sacrifice that includes death at the hands of others, for the sake of others, that we somehow have come to view as good, as holy. It is a pivotal event for Christendom, a marker of how humans betray but God is true and constant, even to and then, we will find out, beyond death.

For myself, the heart of these words that may be of value to us lies in verse 23. The simplest interpretation is that we are to hold fast to God's faithfulness, regardless of what is happening around us. This last evening for our Maundy Thursday event, and then later remembering of the later evening, early morning scriptures indicating that even Jesus asked God to release him from the events of today. Yet, if not possible, let him (Jesus) be steadfast in his devotion to the one who has always been steadfast. On a 'Good' Friday, despite the betrayal of the people around him, the ridicule, the abandonment of all his disciples Jesus stayed the course. We, however, know the rest of the story so our tendency is to see this day as *good*, a necessary step to the Christendom story.

But the reality is this didn't have to happen. The people of Palm Sunday or Maundy Thursday could have stayed faithful. The leaders of the ruling powers, the priests, and the Roman leaders could have said no foul had been committed, no crime committed. The people could have chosen to save Jesus instead of another when given the choice. And therefore, I tend to reject the notion that Jesus had to die to free us from sin. Rather, I think he died because of our sin, and there is no freeing us from it through his witness of steadfastness to God's ways.

We don't get a magical potion of piety that Christ sprinkles on us that cures us from sinful acts, given the many times we turn away from God's ways to pursue our own desires. Perhaps that is why I am not quite as hard on the author of Hebrews for at times it realizes the simplistic formula that Jesus died for our sins is not the only response. Verse 24 encourages us to continue to poke and provoke one another to love and good deeds. Sin is not victorious so long as we continue to rise up against it. Is this thought not of value to us today? Is not the reason we remember a day like today as 'good' and as 'holy' is because we want to be poked and prodded into more love and good deeds?

If the center of our faith, the person of Jesus, was whipped, betrayed, spit upon, nailed to a cross in the most agonizing way, and was recounted in his last words as saying, 'forgive them'…was that not a poke, a prod, to say, *come on folks you can do better, you must do better*?

Is it not a reminder that we nail Jesus to the cross with our every act that turns us away from what he asked us to do…to feed, clothe, give water, visit the imprisoned, love one another, love enemies, not kill, forgive so generously you can't even keep count high enough as if to keep a tally, and be utterly devoted to a life abandoned fully for the sake of others that might end up with you too being abandoned by all?

I think today prods us to both admit our complicity in killing Jesus today just as he was killed 2,000+ years ago, and we must confess that. We kill him by continuing to not follow his ways or pretending that there is separation from needing to follow him in other venues of our lives. We are challenged to understand, that whether Easter came or not, today reminds us, prods us, that we can make a choice. We can make a choice to no longer participate in killing Jesus. As an old confession's words might say something similar, "we are called to turn from our ways, and live."

For myself, since I am retired as a pastor now, I suspect this will be the last time I ever have to preach on Hebrews, thank you Jesus. But I am sure it is not the last time I will be confronted by the cross and its reminder to consider a different way of life. And, to give Hebrews a bit of a nod, even as I have dissed it multiple times in this message already, its call to remain steadfast in a belief that God is with us must never be denied through the way we live our lives.

Amen.

Easter Day
Acts 10:34-43

No Doubt

We finally got here. Easter morning. He has risen! Response: He has risen indeed!

We've gathered; the choir has assembled, and the testimony of scripture is upon us: The story was not imagined. It is real. Christ has been newly set apart so that we too may become set apart! Thanks be to God for the good news. Hope has been heard. Triumph, perhaps differently conceived, has been, well, triumphant!

Even though the epistle is still a little ahead of the game, for it jumps to the accounts we haven't mentioned until today: a tomb being open and empty, a vestige of the body clothes wrapped around Jesus' dead body now laying folded, a messenger telling the women to go and let the disciples know, the confusion they experienced. We are presented with another telling to a group of people of all the Easter events and the meaning of Jesus' life.

The blessing of this scripture this morning is that it is framed not in confusion or curiosity. It is framed in certainty. It is framed for both the gathered faithful and for those who have not yet heard. It holds in its bosom the basics. The good news message is for everyone (v 35), the preaching of peace is for everyone (v 36), the doing of good and healing instead of evil and division is for everyone (v 38), that death is not the end for everyone (v 40), and that those who saw it firsthand offer the assurance of its veracity sufficient enough to proclaim it is so. A new way of life not bound by separation but bound by inclusion is for everyone (v 44). Everyone who believes receives a welcoming community.

I once worked for a senior pastor who thought that the best topic for preaching on an Easter Sunday was the doubting Thomas story. He seemed to feel that everyone who was in church, especially the C and E attendees had doubts about the story of Jesus. Or that those relatives who showed up and attended for "the family's sake" must surely have questions. And, most certainly, he would talk about how it was okay to have questions, never affirming that the story, however told in its many forms, was an affirmation.

As an Old Testament professor once pointed out to our class, her main point was that the greatest things we have going for us in knowing the veracity of the story's essence, Christ is alive, is that there is no seamless, word for word set of words passed down year to year. They are the very process of a people attempting to use the looseness and movement of language to communicate what was seen, heard, repeated. That very fact, she would say, is that by their appearing to be inconsistencies among the writers, rather proved the point that what happened was real. Just as if ten people gathered and saw the same scene of a beautiful sunset or even terrible accident, those who would hear its retelling or see its picture would certainly know it fabricated if all said exactly the same thing. The truth is not in the particular words but in the witnessing of the events, their aftermath, and then the attempt at drawing the meaning of them.

I do not doubt that some in the pews on our holiest of days have questions, just as they do on every day they are in a church. Nor do I doubt that many have left the church because of what they see as inconsistencies in the testimony and might want more conversations (or none because they already made up their minds). But I disagreed with the senior pastor that a message of it being okay to doubt was the right message to preach on Easter. On Easter, the church, both small and big c, is about certainty. There is time enough for questions. Easter is a time for celebrating our *"Yes"* to the news repeated over the millennia and witnessed to through all the experiences through the ages. Other Sundays, share uncertainties, wonderment, quizzical thinking all we want. Yes, the people Peter was preaching to certainly had questions. After all, they were folks who were hearing the message of Jesus for the first time. Yet Peter let us know that first and foremost when addressing those who are unknowing, is the importance of certainty.

He stood forth to preach and teach, that Jesus *was*. Jesus died. Jesus was raised from the dead. His very life and the lives of the disciples are focused on giving that testimony. I know it is what I believe. I know it is what I have seen in the lives of others who follow. I know it is necessary for us to never stop telling the story, telling it on the mountain tops, in the valleys, in the homes and busy thoroughfares we travel. And not only is it necessary, but it is also our responsibility.

Easter is about the gathered community, being clear that we believe. Through all things, in all times, we believe. A creedal statement or a dogmatic injunction on everything about the faith and its meaning is okay. Testimony about why we believe is okay. Or simplicity of celebration with just plain joy and affirmation is okay. It is just a focused time for us to confirm…we believe. We sing…because we believe. We pray…because we believe. We cry together…because we believe. We go into the world…to care for others, to include others, to celebrate others, to overcome divisions amongst others…because we believe. It starts with our affirmation, Christ has risen, he has risen indeed. And we are called to follow. I think it's time for more singing, more praying, more shouting and celebrating the one who has come to us and changed our lives, the living Christ. Blessed Easter to all. May you know fully…Christ has risen. He has risen indeed.

Amen.

Revelation: Behind The Dream

The next six Sundays are going to see us in the book of Revelation as it resides in the lectionary readings for the season of Easter under our Epistle readings. While it has some qualities of a letter to be certain, and historically it has been attributed by some to another letter writer, frankly, most looks into its background are illusive. You've probably noticed that most epistles are targeted to a specific church community and their troubles and challenges with specific suggestions on how they are to be remedied. Then we, as preachers, in turn, attempt to apply the lessons from the past to the challenges of today's church in generality at the least, and at times, with direct one on one comparisons to our situation. But Revelation is a different animal in tone since it is prophetic in nature rather than addressing practical faith applications. Now since we are going to spend the next six Sundays in Revelation, I want to share some things up front.

To begin with, I have an honest confession of my own. There are some scriptures due to uncertainty, dubious authorship, or interpretability that I would just as soon let go of. While they have value to theologians exploring linguistic complexities of interpretation — they are, in my mind, not terribly useful to the average person in the pew who doesn't have the skill sets of a pastor or theologian. Yet the lectionary brings forth the choice of one such book, Revelation, and my task is to see if there are ways to preach the text that can, in the time of the average sermon, do justice to its depth even as its content doesn't make it easy to digest or summarize. And, even more directly, I find that most of the teachings on Revelation that you might know of are usually the worst kind of interpretation and proof texting I can think of. So here are some ground rules for you to think about as you read Revelation on your own and that I will apply to my preaching.

First, think of it more like a picture book, a book of images. Much like a photographer taking a picture, from many different angles, with many different shades of lighting, it calls for us to invest our time in seeing and valuing the images without taking the images as literal. They are symbols for us to "see" but at the same time, explore, and be open to the emotional possibilities present in them. Think of going to an art museum and all the varying portraits on the wall or sculptures on the stands. They are works of art, through the lens of an artist, and yet, they are not, any one of them, the only truth there is on beauty and meaning even as one or more might particularly strike us as profound. We are on a journey through the museum of the mind and emotions that Revelation shares, attempting to try and get a sense of the author's intent. Yet realize that like any work of art it can be viewed from many vantage points.

Two, I see the book as a summative effort, an attempt to bookend the recorded scripture. Much like old time book holders, one on each end of a long line of books, I see Revelation as a counterweight to Genesis. If in the beginning God created the idyllic space according to the biblical story, it makes sense that in the end, God will re-create a new version, a new history of the world and the universe. In the beginning…God. In the end…God. This is something to be celebrated.

Third, I firmly reject that this is some kind of prophetic rendering of a history that the right people, at the right time, can see, interpret, and proclaim that the end is near. Just like a number of years ago when the number one selling book series proclaimed that the end was coming, there was a craze all around their predictions. The world didn't end, as it hasn't during all the other times when the belief that the right interpretation of Revelation could give us accurate predictability that the end time was at hand. It wasn't, it didn't, even as people so wish it.

Even now, with portents of earthquakes, political turmoil, and crises of every kind, I tend to stand with Jesus' words in Matthew 24:36 when we are reminded that no one knows the time, not him, not the angels. And in further caution, he says, it will be on us before we even know it is coming anyway, just like the folks of Noah's story didn't know what was happening until the rain came. In other words, my take is that I can spend all my life in Revelation and guess what, I won't see it coming any better than anyone else, even if I think it is my sole role in life to try and predict the new heaven and new earth promised in Revelation. And while many use fear of the end time to try and motivate folks to accept Jesus, frankly, mostly the authors of end time books get rich, and a lot of people get disappointed. Revelation is not a literal history book, or time-line predictor book.

Having shared these three caveats, I will never make a case that something in the canon of scripture is not worth exploring even if I find all sorts of difficulties with how it is often dealt with in popular culture. If those who found it to be valuable of inclusion into what we call our sacred text, it is my job to attempt to see if there is some value for us in the living of our days. Not to put to blunt an assessment on it all, while I do not think the book merits any attempt to ascertain the very, one and for all ending of this history timeline of humankind, one thing is certain: you and I will all die and be recreated in some form or fashion, whether that ending be of accident or age and maybe even an end time prophetic event. Perhaps, as we look to the bookends of our own lives, Revelation might offer to us something in our journey until that time comes.

Let's begin with the simple words of verse 5. Revelation begins with an affirmation. We are loved. We are no longer bound, but free. What kind of pictures exist in your museum of memories and treasures that you think of that help to remind you that you are loved? For myself it is my wife, my children, my grandchildren. There are the mementos from the many churches I have served with thoughtful comments or a picture of people side by side in ministry. Perhaps my garden that I tend so that the succulent smell of the first flowers in a dew greets my senses could be such a picture. Or even the time I sit with a hospice member of the church, and I see the relaxed look on her face as I sing her the song that talks of amazing grace or recite with her final breaths the Lord's Prayer. When watching the news, the pictures of comfort when following a disaster, a couple recounts that even though they lost everything, the important thing is they have each other affirming a sense of love. We are loved. No more profound thought, emotion…and God loves us. God loved us enough to create us, in the beginning. Now, even in the end, it is revealed that God loves us enough to be fully with us. Despite all the violent images that will be upon us soon in the book of Revelation, the author wants us to first be touched by the image of love. It is love that sees us through.

The second image is one of freedom. Not the kind of freedom that we in America think of in our political foolery or that our rugged individualism is better than any other system. It is a freedom that is tied to love. It is a freedom that is applied in every moment. We are free, regardless of any political system or philosophical system because you cannot bind up love. We are free in the sense that we may love God fully and that in that love, no matter what comes, we are free to center our lives around God. We are free to live in the garden again, at peace, in harmony with all others. It is not about building a wall to keep people out, or even evil out, whether that wall be literal as the fences we build or emotionally as the barriers we put up to being vulnerable and open to others. It is about being free, unencumbered by all the conventions of this world, and working to find a place that connects love and place together as one. And as countless musicians through the ages talk about the trials and tribulations around us, they can be overcome, and we gain freedom from them, through love. While we just finished one of our largest services of the year, and now, only you, the remnant has returned, we get to practice the role of love and freedom that the author of Revelation puts before us.

It would be easy to be discouraged (think "not free" from negative thinking about the picture we see of people who only come on Easter) but rather, the picture I see as I look out among you is one of loving people who care about God…care about each other. The picture we see is one of love, one of freedom to be present, one of understanding the blessing that Revelation's author is calling upon us, even in what will be portrayed as the most heart wrenching of times, the death and destruction of all we are familiar with. But many of you already know that don't you? You've known the heart wrenching times of loss of a partner, or loss of a job you loved, or loss of mobility as you age, or loss of a family member moving away, or loss of a favorite location that filled your youthful filled nights with a place to be, or loss of a Facebook friend who turned on you and made you the butt of their insecurities. You know about heart wrenching times. The author is preparing you…love and freedom go together; they are what will see you through.We will come back to these themes, over and over again, in the pictures of our lives that people travel in and out of, gazing upon, and seeing in us something that either calls to them or repels them. The choice to follow is ours.

The love we show is ours to give that either reflects the love of God or does not. Let us accept the challenge that verse 6 lofty imagery continues with, by becoming the kingdom of priests serving God, with the same love as we have received. That is what we are going to be talking about more concretely in the Sundays ahead than what I want to go into here. But make no doubt…the theme of God's presence in the beginning and at the end is something that we must be grounded in fully. To do otherwise means that we become bound by all the worldly things thrashing around us, trying to get our attention. For me...I want to be worthy of the name priest not as a name set apart for leaders of a church, but in the spirit of a name for all who show themselves in touch with love, showing to all a God that sets us free from worldly things. May others see that in me...may others see that in you. Join me these next Sundays in Revelation in the hopes of finding revelations about ourselves, one another, and how God wishes us to be his ambassadors in the world.

Amen.

Revelation: Praise – A Joyful Name

Have you ever heard someone go on and on about what is wrong with the church? One of the things that many complain about, those who don't attend church anymore, is that they don't like singing or that the singing isn't *hip* to use an old word. And since I'm old I don't know what a current word is to describe the idea that church music should make me want to dance, or celebrate, or move me emotionally. Part of that can be attributed to simple lack of music education that teaches young people how pieces move, or why composers choose certain styles or words to their music so that we automatically listen a little more attentively to all music and can better understand what my participation in it might mean.

My generation was introduced not just to music to listen to, but also to the way music is put together and both how to listen to it, and in many ways, join in singing it in some fashion so that it did not seem foreign. But as those habits faded away, the world of music became more of one of being a passive recipient of it, listening in the background, the radio, and now on all our streaming services, etc. In other words, listening to music over speakers of any kind, where all song is one way making it ever more difficult to use music in worship that is dialogical in nature, both something received as well as given by the worshiper. Song is not an integral part of worship for many. Sadly, that is the exact opposite of what it should be. Even in churches where music style has an important place, too often we tend to fight about what kind of song or what kind of methodology we use to make the song come alive whether a musical instrument or a recording. We let that get in the way of understanding the importance of praise, and how praise is meant to recount the works of God, to recount the greatness of God and to recount how our lives have been moved by the Spirit of God.

Look at what is contained in verse 12. There is a call to singing with full voice, as in, shout it to the mountain tops type voice. The author is reminding us there is no doubt about Jesus Christ. However, back when this scripture was written, as best we can tell, there was doubt. There was worry that the faith was in vain. That evil was all around. That persecution was all around. Questions about how one is to know that God is, indeed going to make it all right, that God has the power to do it is what Revelation is trying to get at. Our part is to offer a full-throated song, or words of praise. Not quiet, in the corner, afraid sufficiently enough to only offer a whisper, but rather song, loud song loud words of joy. It can be the only response to fear. It's all about what has been heard about this person Jesus of just a scant 100 years ago by this witness and the authors testimony that what you have heard is true. Was he really the Son of God? Yes. Is it possible that his life and death had meaning far beyond the average person's life and death? Yes. Is it worth the struggle to stay faithful? Yes.

The recitation of verse 12 in so many hymns and statements that we make are meant to affirm that we are God's people and that we can trust in following God and God's ways. The hope that is derived by this affirmation and this author is that every creature, that every person with voice or a body will in celebration give ascent to the author of all things, God, and through the witness of Jesus Christ our Lord. And like a good congregation when there is the blessed union of good words combined with felt need those who were listening said *amen*.

The bottom line of this selection of scripture is not only about the importance of praise often expressed through music, words, and actions but it is also about understanding that worship is not about us, it's about God. One of the hardest concepts I have ever had a challenge with when it comes to working with all my congregations, is to help them understand that worship is their responsibility. Yes, good music may help it. Yes, favorite scripture readings or the ways in which prayers are said or the type of Lord's prayer that is mentioned may help. Yes, the way in which a style of preaching seems comforting or troubling all have a possibility to aid your worship or in the opening case I described, can be seen to get in the way of worship as in the case of music selection. But do you notice something with my framing of these things. They are focused on your reception of them as seeing them as something presented to you rather than something that comes from you. For myself, I take the position which I think is in harmony with today's scripture: worship, praise of God is your responsibility. It is not something you receive; it is something you contribute. It is something that you do, you worship God for God is worthy of our praise, regardless of what or how someone else does it.

Don't get me wrong, this is not an excuse for those who lead worship, design worship, create worship, or arrange the worship space to be free from exercising their craft in a meaningful way. But the responsibility of worship rests with each of you. You see as preachers, we long ago learned that the sermon that is preached or the worship service that is crafted will find someone going through the greeting line afterward telling us it was the very best sermon or the most precious hymn as well as a person coming through later telling us it was the worst sermon or that they had great distaste for a particular hymn.

You see those very concepts show how personal worship is and even if those comments offer a useful critique on how worship might better be crafted in the future which I hope is their intention, they point to the greater reality that we failed in our responsibility to worship God no matter what is happening around us. No sermon preached or song sung should ever be able to take you out of your worship space, your obligation to give praise to God no matter what is happening. It is our responsibility to be part of every creature's obligation to be singing, that is demonstrating with our wholeness of self, an exuberance for God, regardless of what's happening around us.

When it comes to faith it might be easy for me to point to someone else or something else and say, that disrupted my worship, or did not aid my worship. But scripture does not let us off the hook for being a worshiper. It is our job to say amen and amen, over and over again. It is our task to give praise to God in all situations in all places. It is our sense of love of God that should take centerplace so that we might say, "Worthy is the lamb. Worthy is giving honor, glory, and blessing." Worship is not just a Sunday morning time but all the moments of our lives focused on God so that we might offer praise in every moment and in every place. In the chapters that are preceding this are already words of condemnation, words of the impending judgment to come, and yet as is often the case we are reminded to come back to the basics.

Just as there is worship in the imagery provided as taking place in heaven, we are called to be worshipful here on earth. And even as I accidentally capitalized the word worship in my original writings, I have left it capitalized because I sometimes think that might be a better word than saints to describe the people of faith. It might be worthwhile that rather than talking about the saints of God instead we name ourselves the worshipful ones of God. Revelation challenges us to not go around naive pretending that nothing bad is ever happening or that we aren't to be in the world addressing its challenges and needs but rather it is about our needing to be in an attitude of worship in everything.

A lot of times scripture falls on a communion Sunday for the churches I serve and if this scripture happened to fall on a communion Sunday, I would remind folks that the holiness of the table is no less worthy of our worship than the table that might be set in our homes, might be at the table at a McDonald's, at the table of our car, at the table of our office chairs, or at the table of the sporting events that we watch on TV with snacks close at hand. We are called to be worshipful in every one of those moments; to lead worshipful lives in everything that is ours. The book of Revelation gives us the language that we might share. Worthy is the lamb. Worthy is the lamb. Worthy is the lamb. This Sunday let us go through the week uttering those simple words of worship. See if we can't practice being worshipful ones of our Lord and Savior.

Like other weeks, let me end with a homework assignment. Your task is to practice praising God, and I don't mean saying "Oh, God" when you hit your hand with a hammer"although done in a proper spirit that would be an incredible leap of praise giving. But I mean more so in the following way. Practice praise giving…for your boss, for your partner, for creaking joints, for friends you are estranged from, for the tasks of life that you do most every day, without thought. Let us practice awakening praise in our lives. And yes…write them down. Read what you have written at the end of the day, the beginning of the day, the middle of the day. Rehearse the words aloud, not just in your heart. Revelation says you are created for praise. This morning let us give the great Amen to our worship of God and our worshipful ways of living once we leave this place.

Amen.

Fourth Sunday of Easter
Revelation 7:9-17

Revelation – Put Fear Aside

There has been a lot of commentary in our time about how "fear" works. Fear of immigrants, fear of government, fear of one political party or another, fear of crime, fear of international corporations, fear of AI (artificial intelligence), fear of people of color, fear of electric cars, fear of inflation, fear of losing a job, fear of trans folk... you get the picture. If we acknowledge that basic, what are your fears? While I might offer that as a rhetorical question for the purpose of this sermon, I can also ask it as a real question that would be valuable for you to think about.

There is a lot of fear in Revelation. At the end of chapter six before this morning's passage, there is a whole group of people who have taken to the proverbial hills, hiding in caves, because they are fearful. Perhaps a lot of our behavior as human beings can be explained by our attempts to shut out the world, escape from it in whatever manner we can find. Are we living fearfully? Are we acting like people terrified about what is around the corner, as if in some form of horror flick where everything is seen as potentially jumping out at us and causing our limbs to be severed and blood to be spilled along with our last breath in the most gruesome of ways imaginable? Even as I don't understand the logic behind fear as either a motivator for earthly actions any more than I understand it as having entertainment value, I do understand it as something that pierces our emotional state; that can throw us off balance.

There was a movie out years ago about a shark that terrorized a tourist town. The opening scene was one of a frolicking, young girl throwing caution to the wind, swimming in the water, carefree from any burden. Suddenly the shock of being bitten turns into terror as she is pulled under water and disappears. I didn't get into the water again for a while. Perhaps it also had a bit to do with the fact that in fourth grade, a friend's sister had drowned at the local lake where most of our friends swam for the summer. It wasn't so much the fact that she drowned as it probably was that a substitute teacher leading our fourth-grade class, obviously had not been clued into the grief we were all experiencing and suggested that we all snap out of our doldrums for, 'we all have to die sometime'.

That did not resonate well with this fourth grader whose parents would come in each night and have us recite a version of the prayer we were all taught in some fashion or another: *"now I lay me down to sleep, if I die before I wake, I pray the Lord my soul to take."* Talk about being thrown off balance. I didn't sleep hardly at all for weeks whether in the fourth grade or after seeing that movie as a college student. Thrown off balance to say the least. Even today…I would not choose water as the way to go. And here my country not long-ago chose waterboarding as a form of getting information. Any wonder? Fear works. I suppose that is why, while I never preach fear as a motivator, nor do I believe any preacher should, I can understand the writer of Revelation, willingly putting out there the reality of fear and why it plays an important role in a lot of scripture imaging.

It is not that I wish to put my head in the sand regarding the fears we may have. After all, I once served a church that routinely had hate spewed at it for standing with the LGBTQ community and another that took a stand on women's reproductive rights that had to ask some basic questions on what security measures should we take, including going and hiding in a cave as an option. But in the end our motivation was about wanting to come to grips with the fears that we all have and, in their stead, put in place a resolute faith in God, that God will be with us no matter what.

Here we are, again, in Revelation, after only a few chapters that included fear language and imagery, back at the reminder to worship: be humbled before God, and trust that God's leads us to a safe space that feels like all the fears and tears of life are wiped away. The writer of Revelation wants us to know that for God, this is personal. Notice in verse 13 it talks about the elders addressing the writer directly. The writer was assuring us that it is personal with God. You and I are addressed with a question. Are we following?

Perhaps the question was asked in a threatening tone, but my guess is it was merely a tone of inquiry. Perhaps it was meant as a test, much like a former instructor might ask a former student, now colleague, which never quite takes the edge off the feeling that you are somehow back in the classroom woefully unprepared for the inquiry. But either way, the question is personal. And so, I ask a personal question of you. What are you afraid of? My guess is you've been coming back to it numerous times since I first mentioned it. Why? Because it is a highly charged question. It only took me a moment to recall my friend's sister drowning, or my fear of swimming in regular lake water, ever remembering that when the bluegill fish in the lake playful pull at my leg hairs that it is not a sign of imminently being swallowed up by a shark. And even more easily identified could be the reality of other fears…like, is my preaching acceptable, will I be liked by people, are the forms of my clothing driven by still adolescent fears of acceptance embedded deep within. What are your fears? I'm going to ask you, like I have many other times, to take a moment and jot them down on the bulletin or a piece of paper I've put in the pews. You don't need to let anyone see them. They are for you. What are your fears?

Now that you have them in hand, what's the answer to them? It is the same answer that scripture gives repeatedly. It is the saving, wonderful grace of God. Communicated again in the image of the shepherd or the image of springs of water that quench all manners of thirsting. It is again about the image of God that like a mother comforting a son or a father's arms cradling a daughter, or a grandmother tenderly embracing their grandchild who tearfully takes a chance to tell her they are feeling alone for they do not conform to many of societies prejudged norms. The message is the Lamb wipes away every tear (v 17). Not by changing them, but by embracing them and defeating their fear. God's love surrounds them to make them whole.

Brothers and sisters, do we really need to have the world come to an end to make that real? Do we really need to make that ending something that is far off rather than right now? Just as now, when something horrible happens to a classmate society has learned to bring numerous resources to bear that limit the damage done by grief and terror. Are we not called to bring to bear a love of God that gives witness to the moments of this life, a place where the fears disappear? Perhaps hunger abated, thirst assuaged, abuse put aside, torment by others caged are ways to witness that God's love, in action, is real. Can we not give witness to having a place where we will not live by worldly standard that wants to strip people of their worthiness through all the many fears that are constantly pushed forward as the means of defining them/us, by which our response is measured.

That is why you hear me preach so much about the love and freedom we heard of two weeks ago, being empowered to act as Christ's worshipful ones. People who comfort the afflicted, give food to the hungry, clothe the naked, and visit the imprisoned. It is why we can engage, as long as we have breath in working to bring the image contained in Revelation, of a Christ who loves us, to the now of our lives and to the strangers that we encounter each and every moment. In doing so, the fear of it all drops away and instead a place of coming out of our travails (v 14) has begun. We grow beyond the notion of being afraid of all things into a place of being all right, in the midst of all things, for I am in the hands of God.

Here is an assignment for you. I want you to go home, take that small list of your fears, and get serious about all your fears, no matter how trivial or big. I want you to take that listing after you have done your due diligence and filled it full up. Then tear it up, throw it in the garbage can, for that is where fears belong. And once you have done that, I want you to take some time to pray.

Then call someone you trust and ask them to pray for and with you about those fears and what God will help you in replacing them with. After that, I want you to reengage the world, seeing everything, not through fearful eyes, but worshipful eyes. Giving praise and glory to God, perhaps so completely that many might even think you mad. Make your own revelation of God's love part of your vocabulary and action; don't be afraid anymore. Learn to recognize that when your heart quickens in a situation of fret or unpleasantness, you can defeat the fear it represents, as you are a participant in the most amazing thing of all. God has asked you to be a co-participant in overcoming the fears of the world by bringing a genuine, complete love to each and every one you touch. Just as we respond to the Lamb of God, we are now called to share God's love with all. You are called to pronounce God's care overall. In this scripture, God has spoken to you. Not tomorrow but today. As the church I worship in always ends the service with these words, may it be so. 'Our worship has ended, now our service begins.'

Amen.

Fifth Sunday of Easter
Revelation 21:1-6

Revelation: Think Differently

As we begin to come to the end of the series on Revelation it is worthwhile for us to remember that we often talk about Jesus as the 'good news'. There are times we look around and want to see good news, celebrate good news, initiate good news. But part of the challenge for us is how to do that; how might we be able to get in touch with that good news.

I think some of these closing words in Revelation 21, verse 1-6 can lead us in growing closer to our union with the good news. Chapter 21 starts us right off with the call to a sense of newness. One of the things that we teach our kids is to dream dreams and to have a vision for where they might want to go in this world, what they might want to do, and to be in their journey of life. We engage them in that discussion because we want their lives to be the epitome of good news, at the very least in the ways of this world. To have enough to eat, to drink, to sleep in safety, to find some things they are passionate about and perhaps to be with someone with whom they could share that passion whether at home or at the workplace. It starts when we're dreaming a dream.

Revelation helps us to dream a dream, a new heaven, and a new earth. In the writer's mind, that new heaven and that new earth is captured in the familiarity of a holy city, a Jerusalem, that comes down and is taking the place of an old Jerusalem. It is a place much like an original garden of the creation story with its lushness and its unending plentiful supply of the gracious tastes and sights and sounds and smells of God. It has been transformed into a more modern city of its time. Rather than; being stained of the brutality and the hurt and the pain and the overlords who are in charge of it the new city, the new Jerusalem comes down in its finest adornment, the same kind of adornment the bride is prepared with on a wedding day.

It would be easy for us to fall prey to simple images of what a new heaven and new earth would look like for us today. We are wizened enough and experienced enough that the dream we might dream of that heaven and that earth might be like a city or might be like the mountain valley or might be like the desert oasis or might be like the roughhewn tones of the desert or might be like the stars as seen from a capsule circling the earth where there is no light pollution to cover or hide any part of the glorious stars in the sky. And, as those dreams can and should be part of our imagery, for they are part of scripture, I don't want to limit your kind of dream images whatever they might be. But I do encourage you to think about what is shared in verse 3 and see in your mind the kind of home, and what it looks like, one of God among mortals.

There is a guided devotion that I've often used, in a variety of settings, even in worship in an abbreviated form. I ask people to quiet themselves and I guide them through an exercise: where listening to my voice guide them, they start at their feet, letting the muscle tension go. I move them up through all of their body parts until they get to the very top of their head. Over a ten to fifteen minute period of time, I continue to encourage them to let the tension go. I direct them to imagine the safest place that they know of. Most often people find a place at home, a room or space that is the image that's in their mind and in their heart. It is not a dream as much a profound sense of security, a profound sense of peace. As I continue to guide them through the quieting meditation, I encourage them to see a small light or perhaps feel a gentle breeze that begins to grow in size or feeling. I encourage them to let the sight, the feeling, envelope them. I encourage them to feel like they are being wrapped in a blanket of purity and of wholeness. I encourage them to call upon God; to enter in to surround them with that light, that breeze, to surround them with that peace, to surround them with that blanket of assurance that allows them to, in that moment, experience complete tranquility. I continue throughout encouraging them to let go of anything that keeps them stuck and holding them back so that they can truly feel enveloped by the experience of peace, security, tranquility, calm. Then I just let them rest in it.

It is that very moment when they begin to experience what is witnessed to when Revelation says God is among mortals. It is in those moments when they feel tears wiped away from their eyes, that death has no more meaning, that pain will be no more, for all those things have passed away. They have in that moment and in those moments been able to experience a new heaven and a new earth and they didn't need a dream of some great enchanted place. All they needed was the intent to let go and to let God in.

I find that as I have run this devotional experience through all ages some things of interest happen. One, folks often don't know how long they have been in that moment of peace, thinking it's only a few moments when the reality is we may now be thirty or 45 minutes into the exercise before I begin to call them back to the waking moment. Second, folks almost always realize that much of what they are looking for, defined in terms of 'out there', as a place of newness, is really defined by something more familiar. They didn't have to travel far, after all, to meet God close at hand. Just like we don't have to travel far to experience God close at hand. It is almost like Dorothy in the *Wizard of Oz* clicking her heels and saying there is no place like home; people find that the place where they are most at peace is often a familiar place, a place that feels like home. They find that God is, indeed, there. It becomes an identifying moment of experience in life like a new heaven and a new earth without something dramatic having to happen.

Despite all the terrifying words, images, fears, and trepidations that so much of Revelation brings forward, the one on the throne talks about making all things new. It is not so much about a physical transformation of the space we're in but again comes back to a simple imagery: that the thirsty are given water and not only are they given water that quenches thirst, but they are given water that enables life. That gives the water of life not just physicality, like a cold splash on our face, but it also holds our heart and our mind in a place of refreshment. The scripture that also says the image is done, that God is the beginning and the end, is a reminder that God, the home of God is among mortals. God is not distant from us, God is with us. The imagery is unmistakable. Just as God walked in the garden with the people of the story, Adam and Eve, God, walks with us in the recreation of this world through love and freedom, through worshipful ways of life, giving thanksgiving in each moment, and through our lives dedicated acts of caring for one another. Through agonizing moments of fear and trepidation, God is with us, letting us know that no matter what all things are under God's domain from beginning to end, the Alpha and the Omega.

Like students in a class, the writer of Revelation says to us, write this down. And much like the notes we post on our refrigerator or the sayings that are on the walls that came at just the right time by a friend or a spouse or a child that makes us stop and take notice, the writer says write this down. Why? Simple. It's easy for us to forget that God is with us. Perhaps some of us do need the horror like story parts of Revelation to grab our attention sufficiently. Or perhaps the image of the broken man being lowered through the roof to be healed by Jesus is sufficient. Or perhaps Jesus praying in the garden with tears running down his face and a plea to be freed from what will come will motivate us. Perhaps the beauty of the rainbow, the sign of the promise that God is with us doesn't need to come with terrible destruction. Perhaps at the very beginning the image of a garden, or a scene from our front porch or the transportation we took to gather here today, or the simple act of looking at the bug on the ground as if you're a child seeing something new for the first time or the dandelion growing out of the pavement, they are enough for us to be able to understand and fully embrace that God is with us not just in some future place but in the here and now.

Perhaps the new heaven and the new earth is not something far off but is more like re-opening our eyes for the first time as if coming out of a trance, as if being reawakened so that much like in the devotional exercise I talked about a moment ago, you are called to feel all of yourself from your fingertips to your toes to your heartbeat to the breathing sounds that you make to the rise and fall of your chest and to that wonderful sense that God is with you. I pray it so and I encourage you to take time to let go of all the distractions of this world and to claim the good news, which is with us here and now. Write it down.

Amen.

Revelation: What's Important?

Even though I don't see the Book of Revelation as a book of prophecy in the sense of foretelling, I do see it in the sense of reminding us about what is important. Of great importance is the fact that we tend to forget whose we are: we are the followers of Jesus Christ (the lamb) and God (the father/creator). This is why the imagery in this section of scripture centers around the figures of God/Christ and the image that all emanates from them. And it begs a question. If what is of value and true is the image of hope, what is it that draws us away from that?

What we have found in our broad peak into Revelation and the portions we have looked at through the lectionary schedule is that we become bound by the ways of the world which causes us to either distort the good news of Jesus Christ into a set of presumed morals values and laws that must be enforced upon others or we tend to see the world as not being a relevant agent in God's plans. Our faith becomes stunted, it becomes self-serving, in the fact that it becomes so personal that it's not seen as being relevant in my everyday conversations and in my everyday actions except as they might apply to me and a personal yardstick about what it takes to get me into heaven. In many sections of Revelation, it reminds us over and over, that we are, like the disciple taken to the mountain top to witness the final arrival, that we must be that same witness to God's actions in the here and now. Our call is to let the future take care of itself since, I have noted before, that is what Jesus suggested was the reality.

You might remember that when I began this series, I talked about its linkage to Genesis...in the beginning and book ended with the all in the alpha and omega, the encompassing of everything. This reference in 21:10 reminds us of others taken to the mountaintop, to be in contact with God and God's actions, and then reminded to go down into the valley and give witness to it to others. In Genesis, it talks about creation. In Revelation, it points to re-creation. The challenge of being temporal people of course is that we tend to see things on a time line.

We see life as a series of beginning and endings, and, like the writer of Revelation, the images of our museum portraits of peoples and God experiences, returning to a metaphor I used in week one of this series. We tend to fall into the trap of putting temporal limitations on all things by making them about beginnings and endings on things, even the scripture writers. What's perhaps even more difficult to our condition is that we tend to view what happens between the beginning and ending of the story as being less valuable to explore or seen as independent from the beginning and ending noted in the scripture or our life's story. It becomes too easy to craft a story of inattentiveness to the present moment while focusing only on the beginning and ending. However happy I am that the disciple getting to the mountain top gets to witness the culmination of a re-creation, I think I'd rather be down in the valley, attempting to be a coworker of Christ in the re-creation, here and now, rather than some unknown time in the future.

We have seen how quickly the re-creation can go astray. A look at recent history shows how the church attempts to define the faith, do so in ways that are useful to an outcome that is believed by a particular cultural point of view, in order to promote that point of view. We don't need to go back far before we encounter the point of view that persons of color were seen as less than, not having voting rights, not having civil rights. We don't have to go back far before we encounter the point of view that if you were of German descent or of Japanese descent you were a traitor to our country when a world war broke out and could be put into internment camps or forced to change your language. We don't have to go back very far before we encounter a view that has taken over our religious communities that one has to have a personal relationship with Jesus, or you will be excluded from God's professed community. Just a short 150 years ago, that context of having a personal faith in Jesus was unknown in its current configuration. This idea that Jesus is my friend is anathema to the reality that Jesus is the savior of all.

Our blinders lead us to make of God, of Christ, a final ending equivalent of, to use a football metaphor, a last-minute miraculous play to win the game, rather than showing to all that the creator of all intends for us a life lived in love and hope; a life lived fully engaged in God ways, even as we live in the world. Revelation 22:1-5 is about that very standard for today, not just some time off.

Hear it is again: (vv 1-5) This imagery sounds an awful lot like the creation story were God offers a garden full of plenty where folks will go without want and where all that is asked is that those in the garden will worship and live in fullness with God. Certainly, part of our learnings in that the garden story is the recollection of how we lost that paradise. But Revelation brings it before us again to remind us of what the whole of creation is both yearning for tomorrow and was created for today.

We are called to remember that the opportunity to continue to live with God in the now, in faithful living is not something that is far off. We can be co-creators, re-creators in this world right now, bringing water and the world's brightest crystal to each and every one that we meet. I do not believe that the best use of the book of Revelation is about cataclysmic end or rescue. It is a book of hope, yes, a book that reminds us we can and must act now. Do we really think God wants us to wait and sit aside awaiting some miraculous glorious conclusion to our history and our time? I think, rather, we believe that God wants us to understand that we can gather now, we can worship now, we can see God's face now amidst all those we live with and aside. That it is a now thing rather than a later thing. Rather than, *"get busy, God's coming"*, it is, *"get busy, God is here"*.

Like many things I am not sure how God will really accomplish what today we might call the 'end game'. As I have already testified, I don't take much stock in any attempt at trying to interpret Revelation as a history book full of signs; that if I just have the right attitude or the right clues, I can determine when the end time will be. But I can find comfort, assurance, and hope that God's promise is this: we will never be abandoned, have never been abandoned, and can't possibly be abandoned because it has been witnessed through all the ages that God never let's go. For me that gives me hope that when I walk out the door this morning, when we look at the tasks we have set before us as a church, when we live out what we determined our mission is going to be alongside our brothers and sisters in the world, that perhaps the re-creation has already begun with us.

Amen.

I add this note, that at this point, you might dive into the vision and mission of your church and how it measures up to the standards of being a church that is revealing God's presence and love to all. It seems to me that how my local church is living into the standard of never abandoning others and conduct that reflects that would be applicable. This would be a slightly different way than individual reflection on personal experiences.

Seventh Sunday of Easter
Revelation 22: 12-14, 16-17, 20-21

Revelation: The Invitation Stands

Today is the last day of my series on Revelation. As always, is the end the end or is it merely a beginning or both, at the same time.

From our scripture this morning, the invitation is real, come. Notice the repetition of that word in our scripture this morning. The spirit of the bride said come, and let everyone who hears say come, and let everyone who is thirsty come and it is punctuated by the Lord in these final words of revelation with Jesus saying he is coming, and soon. And the answer is, yes Lord, come.

I am not sure why we have such problems with the word *come*. I mean we like to use it, but do we mean it? There is an old story about how pastors would find someone to dress up like a disheveled, unknown person to come to their church to test their willingness to welcome others even when their motto on the outdoor sign is all are welcome. In most cases I know of where that was tried, most churches failed miserably.

There are the classic challenges that churches have when they say we want young people, we want children — but not if they're crying, disruptive, or talk during worship, and especially if they touch and play with things in the historic lounge that has the very nicest of couches, tables, and lamps, just not for children. And let's not forget to talk about the continuing fact that the greatest hour of segregation in America is still Sunday morning worship.

How much welcoming, coming, is being exhibited when most folks, quite frankly, want to only worship with their own? When I think of all the churches I have served or consulted with, they always think of themselves as friendly and welcoming of others. But the fact is, they are friendly to each other, but a new person coming in is rarely greeted with open arms.

We say come — but come to what, come with what, come how? I think the examples that are given in Revelation lead us into the emotional side of how we are to bring ourselves before God. The language of Revelation that talks about the spirit and the bride telling us to come is a language and image of the joy that should be felt on a wedding night, a joy that should be felt between those who love one another. Revelation says those of you who already love one another and have made a commitment to one another will come. You will come and continue to worship, continue to love, and continue to serve. You will grow in your capacity to love the stranger, the unknown…you will come. In similar fashion, the scripture says to everyone, come. That means we are called to invite everyone into our tent of loving, everyone into our tent of marriage with God, everyone into our tent of being one with God and God's Spirit. It is not a call to come so that they will look like us, behave like us, or act like us with specific mannerisms, clothing, and understandings of the same things in the same way. It is a call simply to encourage us to find oneness in the gifts that God has offered us. Like the values we share in a wedding ceremony, with the two becoming one, it is applied universally that the eight billion shall be extended the call to become one.

As Revelation has done so often these last weeks, the imagery includes that of thirst and water. A need, and a need met. Thirsty all, thirst quenched, all. Unlike the fights that often happen around a water hole in the wild or even amongst people who fight over territory, Revelation is saying all may come, all receive. Don't divide yourselves, don't keep yourselves apart from one another, don't do things that by their very nature separate. Celebrate the diversity that eight billion brings, that the different ways of doing things brings, that the many facets of living in separate lands and separate towns brings. I think the imagery that is contained in verse 20 is a disservice to the here and now if left to stand alone. While yes, we wish the world to be fully reconciled with no more tears forever, we can acknowledge that that wish does not replace the call to come, now. To deal with the call of Christ to give water to the thirsty, food to the hungry, clothing to the naked, visiting the imprisoned, both literally and figuratively has been mentioned before, in many of these last month's messages. That is because the one who testifies to these things says that it is not about some unforeseen time in the future, but that Christ is coming when we ourselves are inviting others to be close, to live fully one with another.

And certainly, we must always be reminded that the implication of the word *come* is not something that is dependent upon another's action, that is, we are waiting for them to come. Rather, it is an imperative for us to go and greet the other person, to go be with the other person, to go into the trenches with the other person and say come with me or even better, let me come with you. Come with me — not necessarily to a place, the church, or not necessarily to another spot, but come with me in this moment in this life that we are living together right now. Think about it this way: think about extending your life through not just going up and saying to someone "will you let me pray with you — will you let me give you a cup of cold water — will you let me engage in this moment of fear, tenderness, or a feeling of hopelessness?" But rather let me come with you and you come with me so that we might walk together in this world. Again, the call of Revelation is very specific: it is about living in a world of hope and of promise. Verse 20 is not something fully done and yet is in the process of being done.

For most of us we are like children in the car — "are we there yet?" When the reality is that we are in the midst of the journey whether the beginning, the middle, or the end of it, in each and every moment. I do think the words of verse 21 put the final stamp on all of our intentions — that grace be with us all.

I believe it is the hope of Revelation for all of us to immerse ourselves in the fullness of the grace of the Lord Jesus. It is not something to be gained later but it is something to live in the now. It means that we have work to do, it means we have the words to do, it means we have the extension of the welcome to do, and it means we have the task of taking all that we are and coming before the Lord, extending that same invitation to each and every one to make sure that their thirsts are met.

As I reviewed this message in preparation to share it with you, I started circling every use of the word come or one of its derivatives. Even I, who regularly repeats things, was surprised how often it came forth. Perhaps it means something after experiencing six Sundays with Revelation. Perhaps it means only that I am tired and ready for the series to come to an end (see how I worked that in?). But perhaps it is a wonderful way to think about Revelation as an invitation. Finding ways to come closer to God. Finding ways to invite others to come closer to God. To just have a closer walk with the one who is all. Oh, I think there might be a hymn using those words! Let's sing praises to God.

Amen.

The Ascension of Our Lord
Ephesians 1:15-23

Feasts Are Good

Note: I would use the ancient practice of the feast day to call the church together for a feast that would begin with some song and this message, followed by a meal. However, you can adapt this message easily enough to fit into a simple order of service.

We will be having a slight departure from our Revelation series for a brief detour into Ephesians for this weekday Ascension Day celebration. The reason for this service is the historically rich remembrances of the Christian tradition even as individual Christian faith communities may not follow them. One such tradition is the routine practice of the ancient habit of feasting days alongside many faith-story remembrances. In our modern culture, perhaps a similarity is the way we gather for a Thanksgiving meal, or a Christmas dinner, or birthday and anniversary celebrations. While I don't want to give the ancient tradition of Christian feasts a secular orientation, these are some of the comparable ways we gather to celebrate in ways that go beyond the everyday meals we consume.

The tradition of the feast day was not symbolic, but full out gatherings, with food, to celebrate events in the faith story. Ascension is one of those many celebrations that fits in between our normal Sundays. Like many of the days, they have counterparts in the Jewish experience, and many are numerically based in relation to other important events. Ascension Day is always the fortieth day after Easter if you start counting Easter Sunday. And for those of you who have paid attention, forty is always an important numerical sequencing, showing that God has done something significant.

For those who haven't followed the habit of an Ascension Day, you need to understand that while there is little to assume that it was part of the earliest church celebrations, it certainly is known to have been well in place by the fourth century. Regardless, food and faith celebrations have always been a key practice of the Judeo-Christian faith communities. Today's message is a nod to the practice of gathering the community, other than on the Sabbath, to remember the great things God has done. So, let's begin.

(reread scripture)

Some pastors have preached the post-Easter texts of how Jesus was continuing to be present, whether walking with followers on the road or whether Jesus was appearing before the disciples or whether Jesus would show up unannounced mystifying everyone. The stories of Jesus presence following the Easter day experience were designed to put to end any doubt that might be had or might remain about the message and meaning of Jesus's ministry.

As we return to one of the Pauline traditions epistles, it is an affirmation that Jesus came to be with us that we might, for one, be confident that Christ wishes us to be in unity with him and secondly, that the call to love others as well as one another comes from God directly. It is not just a nice story about a nice man who lived in a not-so-nice time trying to help people be better people. Rather, the Ascension story is about the affirmation of Jesus's life with us.

The tradition of the early church, when combined with the tradition of monthly feasts of remembrance, gives us an opportunity to celebrate the new life and the new vision for that life which Christ offered to us. This story, and all the stories of Jesus' presence with us on earth, is a reminder of the eternal presence of Christ in the here and now as well as an affirmation, and a reminder of who really has power and dominion in this world. In the presence of such an affirmation, we give thanks. The call for Ephesians for us to give thanks is just that. To give thanks for one another. To give thanks for Christ. To give thanks for the gathered church and church universal. To give thanks for all things so that we might be able to complete the cycle remembered in all the moments of Christs birth, life, death, resurrection, and post-resurrection appearances and ascension.

That was why I suggested that we gather for a feast today after this short message. We gather for a feast because they gathered for a feast. We have gathered to not just eat or exchange pleasantries, but also sing songs, giving testimony of what we have witnessed in our lives that convinces us we too have seen the Christ. We have committed to two hours of being together because the church family has gathered for a family event.

As I have already noted, testimony is an important part of our gatherings even while I recognize in our churches the practice of giving testimony is a challenge. We have talked about it in other sermons. I have provided some ways for you to get started with your testimony, stories of faith, as we gather around the tables that will help you to find your voice. But that is not all we do. Besides the telling of our stories, we will pray together, confess sins, and ask for forgiveness. Using the words of our communion table, talk of breaking the bread together, remembering Jesus' words to be with one another in the symbolism of the bread broken, the cup shared, hoping that our eyes will be opened in all the various ways God has provided an opportunity for us to see.

Here are five questions I would like you to answer. They are printed on the cards, so you don't even have to remember them.

- *One, what is your first remembrance of Jesus?* Did it happen at church, nursery school perhaps? Was it a prayer your parents, grandparents taught? Go back as far as you can to bring it forth in your mind.

- *Two, what is your first memory of death?* Did you feel troubled, secure, confused? Can you account for when and how you became comfortable, as much as any of us can, with death not being the end but just a step on the journey?

- *Three, do you remember your first communion?* What were its circumstances, this thing about breaking bread together? How have you found your experience of the ritual component of the sacrament compared to the feelings of gathering for feasts, whether at home or in a setting like this? Is there a similarity or a disjointedness to them?

- *Fourth, what is the most miraculous thing you have ever witnessed?* How do you think it might compare to being an eyewitness to watching Christ ascend to heaven? And finally,

- *Fifth, If you only had to choose one story of your life to give voice to your belief that God is and is in your life, what would it be?*

As we gather around these tables I will ask from time to time that you talk with one another about how you would answer each of the questions. So, while we are eating our salad…a question. A main course…a question, and so on. This will be one of the few times it will be okay to talk with food in your mouth despite your mother's wishes to the contrary. Let's sing a song now as we move from our worship space to our table space. *(sing, say a blessing over the meal, and begin eating)*

After eating, and all the conversation around the questions, end with this:

> *Friends, before we leave the table, this feast of our Ascension Day celebration, I think we must not let go of the final image in verse 23, the reminder that we are now the body of Christ, that we are to be the embodiment of the Christ in this world to each one that we meet.*

When we think about how Jesus behaved, what Jesus did, how Jesus served, we are called to be that very body now: to each one that we meet and each one that we greet and each one that we minister to and do ministry with. Just as we are blessed to be able to gather around this table and feast together, we are called to gather others around the table and feast with them, making sure that they know the love of Christ just as those who feasted with Christ long ago, experienced his love.

Did you see how natural it was to be together and share our stories with food as the point of connection? We can do this. We can be the body of Christ, we can be under the authority and the power and the dominion of Christ, and we can be rooted in love for others. It is these things that have come from God through the witness of Jesus in our midst, including our remembering of the day he ascended.

We know the rest of the story don't we? He does not leave us alone. The remembering of the Holy Spirit is about to be placed upon us to continue the connectedness to Christ. But for now, let us give thanks for the feast and the telling of our stories of Christ in all his glory and his presence in our lives; the magical things he has wrought in the minutes and hours of our days. Thanks be to God.

Amen.

The Day of Pentecost
Acts 2:1-21

It Is Personal

A note to my fellow preachers:

To be upfront, this is the very first time I have written something this long to be preached on Pentecost. For myself, Pentecost has always been a story perfectly suited for re-creation or enactment experiences — much more so than our more traditional Sundays for reenactment times — like Christmas or Easter, with their jumble of birth and resurrection narratives all over the place and music that becomes widely localized based on country, weather, and cultural customs. Pentecost is largely free from that, at least in America, so it always seemed ripe to me to be a concept that can be dramatized. I'm sure, if you are like me, you can find a variety of dramatizations for Pentecost that include some of the real-world images and experiences that your congregation could use. But my task is simple: where might the text lead us in a way that can allow for at least some words of insight to offer the gathered flock — so here goes.

It is a challenge for so many gathered together year after year to come to a place fresh from all our previous experiences and knowledge of our faith. Few in this place are new to the faith. You have been part of the church's life in any number of ways and have a wide variety of understandings about what it means to believe.

As we look at the scripture in front of us this morning it is about a movement of God, the Holy Spirit, that makes clear the following. One, God's movement in our midst is personal (everyone heard God's intentions in their own language). Two, God's movement is confusing to those who are hearing it for the first time (many voices, many languages defying the logic of normal human interaction). Three, God's movement is old even if experienced in a new way (the repetition of Joel's prophecy and assurance of a new application/affirmation of God's presence. And finally, the calling of all to join in.

Regarding the personal. Sermons are hard. On most Sundays, someone leaves the front door thinking it was the very best message they ever heard, thinking it the worst, or thinking it somewhere in between. If I were to list all the possible ways I have experienced people's reactions to my preaching over fifty years, it would fill up reams of paper. A little of it, frankly, would be something of my doing that deserved either praise or disgust. But mostly, I have learned through the years it says more about the state of the other person's moment in time than anything about me or the scripture. Why? Because God's movement among us is personal. Even in a place where all the people hear the same language, and have relatively common experiences, on that given day, they are in a place, in the depths of their own beings that are very personal. And when I end (or begin) the message with a common prayer of hope that my words or the meditations of all be acceptable to God, it is always a wonderment about how its all going to play out.

Now don't get me wrong. This fact is not an excuse to not try and find the universal theme, the universal understanding for the day that can have meaning for all. But what Acts affirms is that each person experiences God in a unique and personal way. We need not fret about it, but, perhaps, lean into it. Lean into a moment of worship with both different methodologies for expressing God's message and give permission for others to experience God's message in their own unique language. To a degree, we do that in worship: prayer, song, readings, testimony, atmosphere of the space, and the like. But is it enough? Have we, as preachers, really insisted that our congregations develop a wide breadth of ways to experience the faith so that the great 'all' can hear it in their own language?

Regarding confusion. I think that we, as preachers, for all our certainties, are better equipped to be honest about confusion, especially those of us who are not literalists when it comes to scripture. I don't want to be too hard on literalists since I have yet to find any two who claim they are literalists to agree on everything regarding scripture. (See — *it's personal*). But I do think that it is a bit easier, not being a literalist, for me to simply admit that confusion and conflicting experiences can be unsettling. We take unsettledness to be a bad thing. It is not. It is simply something that catches us unaware, and if lucky, it can help us to be open to something we might otherwise miss in our routinized world.

A great deal of my ministry has been in what we call intentional interim ministry. One of the first things one learns is that something very minor can suggest to the gathered folks that something new is about to happen. The simple act of processing down the aisle if the previous pastor always came in by the side door is enough to act like a mighty wind coming across the congregation. Or, if they have never done it before, standing for the gospel reading. Or, when I preach a message on how I feel, the gospel drives us out of our comfort zone and is used as an example. Think about the call for everyone to get up and move to a different seat from the ones they have sat in for five, ten, fifteen, or twenty plus years, including sitting in the choir loft or, oh my, the pastor's chair as a way of seeing differently, unsettledness can result. For all the years I've practiced this exercise, the unsettledness quickly becomes instructive of new insights. Especially when those who were always down in the sanctuary come forward and view their fellow brothers and sisters from up front. Often the observation is one of revelation of how glum they all look!

We must be clear. Unsettledness and confusion does not always yield insight. It can induce fear. And there can be no doubt that many who experience God's movement may turn against it because it is different or a threat to what they see as the way things should be ordered. We must be wise in understanding both the potential for the good as well as the potential of the bad. Just as some would wish I would stay as their pastor. others can't see me leave fast enough so the 'real' pastor gets there. But I think the sense of Pentecost, for the church, is to better lean into unsettledness and confusion as a good sign that God is at work in our lives. We just have to do a better job at trying to discern what that means for us, what the unsettledness is calling us to pay attention to or to do.

The third point I made was that there is an oldness, or continuity, to God that is throughout the ages. The prophet Joel is quoted. It reminds us that God has always promised us new things are coming, even when grounded in the history of what has been. Prophecies, dreams, you name it, life can be full of the familiar and the unexpected. We are part of a journey that began long ago and continues to this day and will even continue into tomorrow unless God deems otherwise. Joel was talking about opportunities to think differently. Whether we are talking about the mission and vision of the church or whether we might be thinking of a vision and the mission of our individual lives, at home, work, play, involvement in the community, God offers an opportunity to be different.

One of the many things I did in my life was to be a jail chaplain. One of the volunteers at the jail had been a former gang member. In fact, he had been a former leader of one of the gangs in the Chicago-land area. As the Holy Spirit grabbed hold of him, he became a new person. He tells the story of how, after his faith awakened, he had to go back to the gang and let them know he was going to be so no more. Part of the ritual of leaving a gang would be to walk down a row as they beat upon you, never certain if you would live or not. He talked about how the beating got harder the more he praised God, being louder and louder in his giving God glory. In the end, the gang members decided they needed to let him leave for fear his conviction of faith might spread to others. Perhaps his story is indicative about just how our lives should also change sufficiently that folks might think that we too are a bit crazy. A bit drunk perhaps to use the scriptures own image. Or even more radical, dreaming new dreams?

Finally, the passage in front of us ends with a simple understanding: *join in*. Perhaps another version of *come*? The invitation has been made. The kinds of invitations that brought you to this church, perhaps a parent's request, the need for words of affirmation that you are loved, the need to be joined in union, the need to be sheltered from abuse, the need to find a quiet and secure place, a need to fall on your knees in confession, a need to praise, repeatedly until you are lost in the ecstasy of joy, a need to break bread together with others in a feeling of wholeness around a table that is welcoming and loving. All of these invitations and more — we are called to invite all into an experience that affirms God is near. God loves us. God encourages us. God speaks to us in ways that drive us forth into the days ahead with a passion and a certainty, just as the early disciples felt it. May what they experienced be what we experience even if our words are different or our calling in life is different. Let's be open to be driven out of this place into the world of God's possibilities when the 'rushing wind' comes over us.

Our doors are about to be open to let the summer air in again. When you feel it, perhaps, just perhaps, you will have an inkling, however small, that God is touching you, just like the wind on your cheek, so be ready to act on behalf of the one who is the Alpha and Omega of all.

Amen.

About the Author

Reverend David Plant has been working in churches since 1968 in a multitude of settings — youth pastor, associate pastor, senior pastor, in both settled pastorates and interim pastorates. He has been a jail chaplain, a director of alumni relations for his college, been elected to political offices, and sat on numerous non-profit boards.

His ministry has extended over three states, 23 churches, and he has held numerous voluntary positions in his denomination's judicatory settings. David received extensive training in Systems Thinking and Church Revitalization work, which he extensively used to help congregations during times of transition and as part of a training team equipping over 100 churches in models that develop healthy, thriving congregations.

As a lifelong member of the United Church of Christ, a graduate of The Methodist Theological School in Ohio, and Defiance College, Defiance Ohio, he is married to the Reverend Doctor Marian Plant, a specialist and professor, now retired, in the field of faith formation. They have two grown children, Joel and Jordan, who they are blessed to have living in the same town with them, along with a wonderful daughter-in-law, Christi, two grandchildren, and a myriad group of cats and dogs between them all.

While retiring from active parish ministry in December of 2022, he still fills in on occasion at his local church and works as an annuitant visitor to retired UCC clergy in his geographic area. He tells us he has refrained from boring us with his golf and gardening stories, which are his favorite past times, but makes no promises about his other favorite pastime, talking.